A Soldier's Life

A corporal of the Northumberland Fusiliers with a lance corporal of the Durham Light Infantry, standing outside the artillery entrance to Newcastle Barracks, on Barrack Road, c.1898.

(From an original painting by James Alexander of Ashington.)

A Soldier's Life

The Story of Newcastle Barracks
established1806

Thomas L. Hewitson

tyne bridge
publishing

Newcastle Libraries & Information Service gratefully acknowledge the support of the Sir James Knott Trust in the production of this book.

Photographic acknowledgments:
All photographs are copyright of Newcastle Libraries & Information Service unless otherwise indicated in the text.

The cover illustration is from an original painting © James Alexander, 1998.

Drawings reproduced on pages 7, 27, 34, 56, 70, 72, 87, 88 © Kemi, 1999.

The back cover illustration is from a postcard sent in 1917 (author's collection).

The extract from *Tommy* by Rudyard Kipling is reproduced courtesy of Methuen.

©Thomas L. Hewitson, 1999

Published by
Tyne Bridge Publishing
City of Newcastle upon Tyne
Education & Libraries Directorate
Newcastle Libraries & Information Service, 1999

ISBN: 1 85795 099 2

British Library Cataloguing-in-Publication Data: a Catalogue Record for this Book is available from the British Library.

Printed by Bailes the Printer, Houghton-le-Spring.

Contents

Acknowledgments

I have contacted a great number of regimental museums and headquarters throughout the United Kingdom while carrying out my research, with varying degrees of success. Those who did reply were extremely helpful and I would like to express my appreciation for the time they spent searching their records. I should also like to express my thanks to the Trustees of the Royal Northumberland Fusiliers Museum for permission to quote from *St George's Gazette*, the former regimental magazine of the regiment, which was a unique publication. Without access to the information contained in the volumes it would have been almost impossible to produce this record of Newcastle's own barracks.

There are so many people to whom I owe a debt of gratitude for their unstinting assistance in my research. Mrs. Marion Harding of the National Army Museum. Brigadier D. Hodge DL; Colonel M.D.C. McBain (now deceased); Brigadier J.F.F. Sharland; Lieutenant Colonel D.R. Summers; the staff of Ashington Library, and Anna Flowers and the staff of Newcastle City Library for their unfailing courtesy.

A big thank you to my fellow enthusiasts, and some old friends. Jimmy Alexander; Dick Brown; Ann Scott Bull; 'Chuck' Chambers (ex-RNF, now deceased) for permission to use his photographs; 'Trish' Bailey; Colonel Charles Baker-Cresswell (ex-RB, RNF & RRF); Bill Beattie and his wife Doreen (ex-RNF & RRF) (see appendix); Sara Campbell, my mentor; Mick Fellows; Jack Herdman; Harry Moses; Don Price; Captain Bill Pringle and his wife Alice (ex-RNF & RRF); Ralph Thompson; Major Dennis M. Thornton and his wife Margaret (ex-RNF, RRF, RAR UDR & MOD) and their son Staff Sergeant Michael Thornton, RAMC; Malcolm Wall; Jim Winter; Colonel Denis Wood (ex-RNF & 2nd Goorkhas); for their active support and encouragement.

Finally I would like to express my gratitude to my wife Ada, for her forbearance and putting up with all the extra work I gave her when I had our home littered with books, photographs and documents, and my frequent trips up and down a creaking metal ladder into our loft looking for references; it always seemed to be when she was watching her favourite television programmes.

Thomas L. Hewitson, 1999

Dedication

This book is dedicated to the memory of James and Basil Knott, both of Newcastle upon Tyne, who were killed in action during the Great War of 1914-1918. Without the assistance of the Sir James Knott Trust, which was set up by their father to perpetuate their memory, this record may never have been produced.

It is also a memorial to the men, women and children who have lived and worked within the barracks walls since they were first built; all those recruits who passed through the barracks, volunteer and conscript alike, while in the service of their country; some never to return to their homes.

Also to Staff Sergeant Michael Thornton, the Royal Army Medical Corps, presently serving within the barracks as an Permanent Staff Instructor with the Territorial Army; a soldier from a soldier's family.

Tommy

We aren't no thin red 'eroes, nor we aren't no black-guards too,

But single men in barricks, most remarkable like you;

An, if sometimes our conduck isn't all your fancy paints,

Why, single men in barricks don't grow into plaster saints;

While it's Tommy this, an' Tommy that, an' 'Tommy, fall be'ind,'

But it's 'Please to walk in front sir,' when there's trouble in the wind,

There's trouble in the wind, my boys, there's trouble in the wind,

O it's 'Please to walk in front, sir,' when there's trouble in the wind.

Extract from 'Tommy' by Rudyard Kipling (1865-1936)

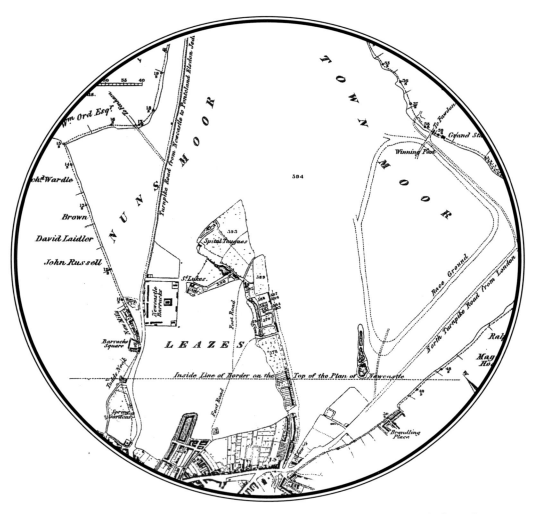

Newcastle and its barracks from Thomas Oliver's map of 1830. At this time the barracks were surrounded by farmland.

Introduction

My initial reasons for compiling this account of the old barracks in Newcastle were a mixture of nostalgia and curiosity. It was not until I started my research that the impact that the barracks has had over the years on the military, political, economic and social history of the city of Newcastle upon Tyne became apparent to me. The history of the barracks, or what is left of them, also reflects the great Victorian age and the rise and fall of the greatest empire that the world has ever seen. It also occurred to me that, as far as I am aware, there is no definitive account of the story of the barracks and the men, women and children who dwelt within the barracks walls.

Having done my basic training in the barracks, after being called up for National Service with an infantry regiment, they have a personal interest for me. It is also highly likely that a very large proportion of the citizens of Newcastle upon Tyne have never seen, or know of, the barracks on the edge of their city. Nor will they know of the involvement in the life of their city of the soldiers from the numerous regiments who have been based in the barracks over the years since 1806.

Northumberland, and I include the city of Newcastle upon Tyne within this area, has always been a turbulent county prone to devastation by wars and the effects of political and social dissent. Newcastle was always the military rendezvous for the English armies on their way to fight against the Scots. It is no accident that the county has more castles and remains of military defences than any other county in the United Kingdom. The most ancient of all, of course, is the Roman Wall, although it is worth considering the fact that most of Northumberland lies to the north of the wall. But of them all, the military establishment that best reflects the rise and fall of a great nation, within our remembrance, is the barracks in Newcastle; or, as it is better known today, Fenham Barracks.

There can be no doubt that the fortresses in the North East of England were constructed purely for defence, especially the Elizabethan walls built at Berwick upon Tweed to deter the Scottish armies. Berwick has the distinction of having the first purpose built army barracks in England, constructed in 1719-20, while those on Holy Island, Tynemouth Castle and Clifford's Fort at the mouth of the River Tyne, and Sunderland Barracks at the mouth of the River Wear, were for the defence of the coastline and the ports against seaborne invasion.

During the Napoleonic Wars (1793-1815) large numbers of troops were based on the coasts of Northumberland and Durham to guard against invasion by French forces, because of the enormous importance of the North East coalfields. Even before the age of steam, large quantities of coal were taken by sea from Newcastle to London and other ports in the south of the country. In 1791 for instance, the quantity of coal shipped to London from the ports of Newcastle, Sunderland, Blyth and Hartley, was 790,673 Newcastle chaldrons (one chaldron equalled 53 hundredweights). This amounted to just over 39,533 tons. In May 1800, the total number of vessels engaged in this trade from Newcastle and Sunderland was 597.

But there was another reason for the presence of the barracks and its soldiers. The last quarter of the 18th century had seen two revolutions: the American Revolution in 1775, and the French Revolution in 1789. The effects of these events were being felt in Great Britain. Urged on by wealthy landowners, coalowners and businessmen, the Lord Mayor of Newcastle made an application to the Home Secretary in 1793 to have a barracks built in the town; ostensibly as an ordnance depot, but in reality as a means of social control. This was so that the troops based in the barracks could be (and were!) used on occasions to subdue the citizens of Newcastle and the surrounding area during times of social and political unrest in an age before the introduction of formed and disciplined bodies of civilian police. This unrest was manifested in the strikes of the seamen and keelmen of the River Tyne, militia riots, food riots, the political agitation, in the 1830s and 40s of the Chartist movement (a radical political group seeking a more democratic system of government) and frequent pitmen's strikes.

The peak periods for Newcastle Barracks were, quite obviously, the years during which Great Britain was involved in major wars; South Africa (1899-1902), the Great War (1914-18), and World War II (1939-45), with the consequent expansion of the armed forces. With the end of World War II, and the gradual withdrawal from the British Empire which led to the ending of National Service (conscription) in 1960, large numbers of barracks that had been built during the 18th and 19th centuries became redundant. Among them was Newcastle (Fenham) Barracks. The resultant demolition of the old barracks and the construction of a business park and student accommodation for Newcastle University, has meant that at least one part of the barracks' contribution to the City of Newcastle, the economic part, has not been lost. The main military presence in the barracks today is that of the Territorial Army. Such is the process of change that the descendants of the people to be contained by soldiers from the barracks, now occupy the barracks themselves as citizen soldiers.

Sir,

It has long been our opinion that the peace and good order of this part of the country would be more effectually preserved if the civil power had within its reach, on the shortest notice, the assistance of two or three troops of Horse.

We are now urged by the general sentiments of the inhabitants and of the parties interested in the coal trade to request Their Majesty's Ministers to direct that barracks for Horse may be built in this town or its neighbourhood. The present turbulent disposition of the sailors of this port and the tumultuous spirit which, on several occasions, has recently shown itself among the pitmen and others employed in the coalworks appear to us strongly to enforce the propriety of adopting this measure.

We wish to express a high sense of the obligation the country owes to the troops which were directed on those occasions, to give aid to the Magistrates.

We have the honour to be Sir,

With great respect your most obedient and humble servants.

James Rudmann, Mayor.

The Right Honble., Henry Dundas.

Newcastle upon Tyne
28 March 1793.

1 Newcastle and its Barracks 1806-1877

Barrack: A hut, like a little cottage, for soldiers to live in, those of the Horse were called Barracks, and those of the Foot, Huts; but now the name is indifferently given to both. They are generally made by fixing four strong forked poles in the ground and laying four others across them; then they build the walls with wattles, or sods, or such as the place affords. The top is either thatched, if there be straw to spare, or covered with planks, or sometimes turf.

Definition given in 'An English Military Dictionary', published in 1702.

Except for royal fortresses there were no permanent barracks in England until the end of Queen Anne's reign (1665-1714) and this resulted in the highly unpopular billeting system. However, after 1689 the billeting of soldiers in private houses, except in emergencies, was forbidden by an Act of Parliament. Instead, the Act stated that they were to be accommodated in: 'Inns, Livery Stables, Ale-houses, Victualling houses, and all houses selling Brandy, Strong-Waters, Sider [sic], or Metheglin [sic] by retail … and no private houses whatsoever.'

This Act, however, caused problems for the owners of the premises listed. So unpopular were soldiers that in some cases they simply closed their establishments rather than have soldiers billeted upon them; and some gave up their licences to trade. The situation became serious for the innkeepers in the area around Newcastle upon Tyne at the end of 1794 and early in 1795, when cavalry moved into the district during a dispute between pitmen and their employers. The *Newcastle Chronicle* in March 1795, states that one Newcastle publican was losing between 30 and 40 shillings per day (£1.50p to £2.00), a great deal of money at that time, because of the troops billeted on him. Innkeepers as far away as Morpeth and Hexham, in Northumberland, were also affected. The great demand for hay for the cavalry horses had caused an increase in prices. At Hexham it reached a higher price than ever before, and it was rumoured that farmers were hoarding their hay until the prices rose even higher.

A delegation of innkeepers from Newcastle met General Balfour, commanding the Newcastle Garrison, and pleaded their case. The general told them that if those who wanted the cavalry in the area did not contribute to their support he would take steps to remove the cavalry. Meetings were held with the gentlemen of Newcastle to find ways of helping the innkeepers and a subscription was opened, out of which each innkeeper would receive sixpence (2¹/₂p) per day for each horse stabled with him. It appeared that donations to the fund were rather meagre.

The first purpose built barracks in England were Ravensdowne Barracks in Berwick, Northumberland, designed by Sir John Vanbrugh and completed in 1720. In 1758 temporary barracks, later demolished, were erected at Clifford's Fort, Tynemouth, to house one thousand men. However, billeting went on well into the 20th century. In fact, on 21 September 1885, men and horses of the 4th Hussars, on their way to Edinburgh by route march to relieve the Scots Greys, were billeted overnight in public houses in Alnwick, Northumberland, the officers in the White Swan and two warrant officers in the Star and the Nags Head. Billeting was again used during the 1914-18 and 1939-45 wars.

Such was the universal dislike of billeting that it was decided by the government of the day to embark upon a programme of barrack building. In 1792 the Prime Minister, William Pitt the younger, created the post of Barrackmaster-General, responsible for the construction of permanent barracks throughout the Kingdom – not without opposition however. The idea was seen by opposition Members of Parliament as a potential for military repression, and as late as 1812 one MP, Samuel Whitbread, asked if barracks were to be '… fortresses for controlling the citizens?' and another MP Sir Francis Burdett, said '… the object of [the] Government in erecting barracks all over the country is that they might use the troops paid by the people to subdue the people.'

The first holder of this post was Colonel Oliver Delancey (late 17th Light Dragoons), which turned out to be a controversial appointment. He was blamed for the misappropriation of a large portion of the public funds allocated for the building of barracks, and accused of lining the pockets of friends and cronies by appointing them Sub-Barrackmasters in places where there were no barracks and none planned. A report in the *Newcastle Courant*, of 26 April 1806, states:

The first report of the commissioners of military enquiry, respecting the barrack department, has been printed. It represents the late barrack-master general, Lieutenant General Delancy as being indebted to the public for no less than £97,415,00. Of this sum £88,923,00 was appropriated by himself, by General Delancy as indemnity for contingent expenses; to which he had no claim.

In the year 1792, barracks were set up in rented accommodation in Morpeth, Tynemouth and Seaton Sluice. A great number of regular and militia regiments were on coastal defence in Northumberland and Durham, and were quartered in billets and tented encampments. In Newcastle in the same year a proposal was made that a barracks should be built and paid for by public subscription; this idea was not proceeded

Newcastle, 1823. A soldier, probably from the barracks is in the foreground. (Newcastle upon Tyne by J.M.W. Turner, published as part of 'Rivers of England', June 1823)

with. Instead, in 1793, James Rudman, the Lord Mayor, and the Corporation of Newcastle petitioned the Home Secretary, Henry Dundas, to have a Cavalry Barracks built in the town.[1]

It was not until 18 April 1804, that an agreement was signed between the Incorporated Companies of Newcastle and a Government Agent, for 11 acres of land to the north of Newcastle, near Spital Tongues, at an annual rent of £55 to create a large depot for military stores, barracks, stables etc. The barracks were designed by James Johnson and John Saunders, who were responsible for the design of most of the barracks in the British Isles in that period, and the building of this depot was completed in April 1806 at a cost of £40,000.[2] When finished, the barracks could accommodate one field officer, three captains, six subalterns and 264 soldiers, with stables for 294 horses. The 21st Light Dragoons, which regiment is mentioned in the local press on Saturday 11 January 1806, as being on the march from Woodbridge to Newcastle, stayed a very short time in the town. An item in the *Newcastle Courant*, 19 March 1806, mentions that: 'The troops of the 21st Light Dragoons which was stationed in this town have marched for Sheffield and part of the North British Dragoons (Scots Greys) have arrived in their room'.

Since the barracks were opened in April 1806, it seems likely that this unit would have been the first to occupy the new quarters.

The barracks were built of brick to a standard pattern consisting of two-storey buildings with the men's quarters on the first floor, reached by an outside iron staircase. The horses were stabled below the barrack rooms. Two copper boilers were

Chimney Mills, Spital Tongues from an engraving by T.M. Richardson.

issued for each room, one for meat and one for vegetables. Sanitary arrangements would have been equally primitive. In fact, out of 146 barracks in Britain at that time, 89 lacked any washing accommodation for men and 77 had no facilities for washing clothes. Water would usually be drawn from a pump, or well, in the barracks.[3]

Separate latrines and ablutions did not appear until well into the 19th century. Each room was issued with a urine tub for use during the night, but this was sometimes kept on the outside landing. As well as these rather unsanitary arrangements, wives and families of serving soldiers were expected to live in a corner of the barrack room; sometimes only partitioned off by a blanket or paper screen. However, by 1822 the accommodation had been increased to house 770 soldiers.[4]

Army regulations of 1822 give explicit instructions to officers and soldiers as to the way barracks should be run, including such details as: 'The general practice of Washing the Floors of Barrack-Rooms having been found very prejudicial to the Health of the Soldiers, by exposing them to a damp Atmosphere, this pernicious custom is to be discontinued, and Dry Rubbing is to be submitted in its place.'[5]

Perhaps it was this order that led to the practice of frequent polishing of wooden floors. From personal experience in 'Y' Squad, Recruit Company, the Royal Northumberland Fusiliers, from September to December 1953, every Friday night was spent applying liberal quantities of floor polish, then laboriously polishing the floor to a mirror like finish with a very heavy bumper.[6]

It would seem that life in the barracks, and, perhaps, soldiering in general, must have been a depressing existence, in what was a hard and brutal age. One of the 'diver-

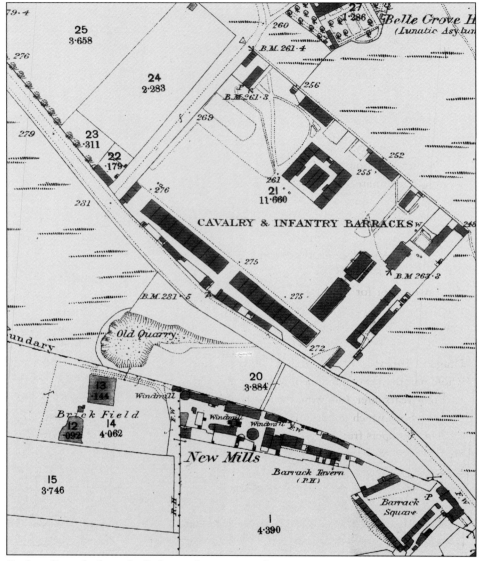

Fenham Barracks from the Ordnance Survey map of 1858-59.

sions' that the troops in the garrison would have access to would have been the public hangings that took place on temporary gallows on the Town Moor, not very far away from the barracks. Among those hung were: John O'Neill, 7 September 1816, for robbing George Angus; Charles Smith, 3 December 1817, for the murder of Charles Stewart; and Jane Jameson, 14 March 1829, executed for the murder of her own mother. Apart from the spartan life style, and the harsh discipline which included flogging for various breaches of rules and regulations, alcohol played a large part in most soldiers' lives.

During the research for this record, numerous instances of soldiers committing suicide have been found. The *Newcastle Courant,* 27 June 1807, contains a report of one instance: 'On Sunday morning last [21st] Robert Moor, a corporal in the Inniskilling Dragoons, shot himself through the heart in the Rose and Crown in the Bigg Market, in this town. He arrived from Rothbury only on the Friday preceding and appeared melancholy from the time of his arrival.' Two troops of the 6th Inniskilling Dragoons had arrived in Newcastle on Thursday 15 January 1807, and another two troops on Monday 18 January.

The 4th Dragoon Guards were also in the barracks in 1811, when another soldier was more fortunate. Fordyce's local records tell us that: 'While exercising in the Bigg Market on 12 March 1811, a dog bit one of the troopers' horses, the horse reared up and fell over, and bursting a blood vessel bled to death. The trooper was unhurt.'

Another indication of the numbers of regular, militia and volunteer regiments stationed in and about Newcastle during the period of the Napoleonic Wars is given in a description in the *Newcastle Courant,* 6 June 1812, of a ceremony which took place on the Town Moor for the birthday of King George III: 'On Thursday last [4th] on the King's birthday, ten regiments of volunteers commanded by Lieutenant Colonel Rawdon, were reviewed at noon on the Town Moor by Lieutenant General Sir Charles Greene. They fired two volleys in honour of the day. Also on parade were the 2nd Dragoon Guards and a Brigade of Royal Artillery with eight 6 pounder guns. The whole parade was commanded by Major General Murray.'

Eight years later, following the death of George III in 1820, it was the band of the 6th Dragoons which led a procession of the Lord Mayor and other officials, with an escort of troopers from the Dragoons stationed in the barracks, to the Sandhill where the accession to the throne by King George IV was proclaimed.

Newcastle Barracks as it was in c.1910. In the left foreground can be seen the gardens of the officers' mess. On the left are the original barrack blocks built in 1805. (Photo: T.Hewitson)

The Fruit and Vegetable Market in the Grainger Market in 1841.

The first half of the 19th century was a time of great social and industrial unrest in the North East. A notable year was 1831 – a particularly turbulent and violent time for the coal mining industry. The miners' annual bondage contracts had expired and they refused the terms of the new ones. Accordingly, on 5 April the miners in Northumberland and Durham went on strike. There were violent clashes with the strikers at Blyth, Bedlington, Cowpen, Netherton and Jesmond Dene Collieries. Troops from the barracks in Newcastle were stationed in the area around Wallsend. In Durham, the Lord Lieutenant called out the Northumberland and Newcastle Volunteer Cavalry. They were replaced by regular cavalry of the 3rd Dragoons from Newcastle, and soldiers of the 82nd Foot (2nd Battalion, the South Lancashire Regiment 1881) from Sunderland Barracks were stationed in the Hetton area for some time. A Royal Navy sloop, with a detachment of eighty Royal Marines, was sent from Portsmouth to the River Tyne, where the marines quelled a disturbance at South Shields colliery. By the middle of June the miners had accepted the new conditions.

One soldier who served in Newcastle Barracks during 1834-35, was Colour Sergeant George Calladine of the 19th Foot, (1st Battalion, the Green Howards 1881) who alternated between Tynemouth Castle, Sunderland and Newcastle Barracks. He kept an account of his service and in it he describes many events that took place in Newcastle and the surrounding district. He also describes one of the other units which served in the barracks during his time.

According to him: ' ... The Scots Greys were stationed here with us, and a fine body of men they were, but terrible drunkards ... '[7] He tells of the General Election in January 1835 when his company and the depot had to march to Tynemouth while voting took place in Newcastle, and marching back to Newcastle Barracks on 14 January when the election was over. In the October of that year he describes the opening of the Grainger Street Market which impressed him enormously '... the Saturday following it was opened for business, and I had the pleasure of going through it. I never saw anything like it before, and I don't suppose I ever shall again.'[8]

On 28 October 1835, Calladine's regiment left Newcastle for Stockport and he writes: ' ... and must needs say that I left the north of England with regret, after having been at Sunderland, Tynemouth and Newcastle three years and a half.'[9]

Marching in and out of the barracks, Calladine and his fellow soldiers must have been familiar with the windmills which were opposite the entrance. These windmills are shown on maps of the period and also appear on a watercolour painting by Henry Burdon Richardson, the son of Thomas Miles Richardson the well known Newcastle artist. The painting, *View from the Barrack Walls on the Leazes, Newcastle upon Tyne*, was donated to the Laing Art Gallery in Newcastle by W. Bruce Reid.

On 28 June 1838 cavalry of the 5th Dragoon Guards, and infantry of the 52nd Foot, (2nd Battalion, Oxfordshire and Buckinghamshire Light Infantry 1881) were called out from the barracks to disperse a rally of Chartists (campaigners for political reform) at the junction of Westgate Street and Collingwood Street, after the reading of the Riot Act.[10] The Riot Act was a statute passed in 1715 (the year of the first Jacobite Rebellion) by which persons committing a riot had to disperse within one hour of a magistrate reading the Act. The cavalry patrolled the area until midnight. As a result of the political agitation of the Chartist movement, which was particularly strong in the north, troops were regularly called out from Newcastle Barracks in aid of the civil power.

Chartist agitation was the cause of armed troops being on the streets of Newcastle again on the evening of Tuesday, 30 July 1839. One troop of the 7th Dragoon Guards, and two companies of the 98th Foot, (2nd Battalion, the Staffordshire Regiment 1881) from the barracks, under the command of Lieutenant Colonel Campbell, came down Westgate Street to break up a Chartist rally which had marched from the Forth via Collingwood Street, Westgate Street to the end of Spital.

The 98th Foot left Newcastle with a flourish. Lieutenant General Sir Charles Napier presented the regiment with new Colours at a spectacular ceremony on the race course on the Town Moor in front of a large audience of townspeople on 10 May 1841. In the evening the officers gave a grand ball and supper to 230 guests in the Assembly Rooms.

Another body of troops which occupied the barracks was composed of the four depot companies of the 87th Foot, (1st Battalion, the Royal Irish Fusiliers 1881). In

1831 orders had been received to split the regiment into four depot companies, and six service companies which were sent abroad. On 5 May 1841 the four companies made their first journey by railway, travelling from Carlisle to Tynemouth, where they were quartered in the castle. On 2 June they moved to Newcastle, one of the towns in which the Chartists were very active. Lieutenant General Sir Charles Napier was then commanding the Northern District where most of the trouble was expected, but in June there was trouble in the 87th Foot itself. Napier wrote: 'The Aigle [Eagle] Catchers have been making a row at Newcastle. In my opinion Irish regiments should not be commanded by Irishmen, they get on better with others. Major [Magennis] won't let a soldier speak to him unless brought up by a non-commissioned officer! And now when some of his men behave ill he is absolutely encouraging them in outrage.'

The row that Napier noted had occurred early in the afternoon of 7 June 1841. Several men of the 87th were drinking in public houses in Sandgate, and at about 8pm in the Green Tree, Mrs M'Gallon, [sic] the landlady, had to call the police to clear out some of them who were very drunk. One soldier was picked up and taken out, and when his comrades saw this they set about trying to release their friend from custody. The upshot of it all was that the affair ended in a riot during which, at one stage, there were at least 5,000 people assembled. The trouble took a great deal of sorting out, and left a long period of bitterness between the townspeople and the army.

The 87th left for Hull, with one company detached at Scarborough, on Friday, 25 July 1841. They were relieved by the 10th Foot, (the Lincolnshire Regiment 1881) who

The Assembly Rooms, Westgate Road, the venue for the Officers' Ball of 1841.

were in turn relieved a month later by the 61st Foot, (2nd Battalion, the Gloucestershire Regiment 1881). Some soldiers from this regiment also seemed prone to trouble. According to the *Newcastle Courant*, 4 November 1842, there were ten soldiers of the 61st in Newcastle Gaol, and on Friday 28th, '... they refused to perform their allotted labour, alleging as the grounds of their discontent that the oatmeal served out to them was of inferior quality.'

It was not all dull barrack routine, with occasional forays in aid of the civil powers against the citizens of Newcastle and the surrounding countryside, who were demonstrating for social and political reform. There were times when ceremonial occasions, which the British army has always presented with superlative expertise, were held attracting thousands of people to see the pageantry and spectacle. One such event was the presentation of new Colours to the 37th Foot, (1st Battalion, the Hampshire Regiment 1881).

The ceremony took place on the Town Moor (within the circle of the racecourse, nearly opposite the grandstand) on 12 July 1843. An account in the *Newcastle Journal*, 15 July 1843, tells us:

Headquarters and two companies from Newcastle Barracks, two companies based in Sunderland Barracks, and three companies based in Tynemouth Castle paraded on the moor; with the outlying companies being brought into Newcastle by train. The ground was kept by a squadron of The 8th Irish Hussars, with a detachment from The Royal Horse Artillery under Lieutenant Colonel Higgins. The Colours were blessed by the Reverend William Dood MA, incumbent of St Andrew's, principal chaplain to the Garrison. General the Honourable Sir Alexander Duff GCB, who had stayed overnight in the Queen's Head, presented the Colours to the battalion.

The Grandstand on the Town Moor racecourse c.1840. It was burned down in 1844.

Five tents were erected in the barracks, with a separate tent for the wives and children, by Mr Balmbra of the Wheat Sheaf in the Cloth Market, in which the troops were entertained after the ceremony. In the evening a ball took place in the Assembly Rooms in Westgate Road, where the officers of the regiment entertained 300 guests. Not to be outdone, the sergeants held a ball in a marquee erected on the barrack square, and 2,000 yards of calico were used to decorate it. To close the festivities a firework display was held in the barracks late in the evening.

The 37th Foot were relieved by the 36th Foot, (2nd Battalion, the Worcestershire Regiment, 1881). Shortly after moving into the barracks the commanding officer, Lieutenant Colonel Archibald Montgomery Maxwell, died very suddenly. He was given a most spectacular military funeral, the likes of which had never been seen ' ... within the recollection of the present generation ...' *Newcastle Courant*, 30 May 1845.

A picture of Newcastle Barracks emerges from a House of Commons return dated 14 August 1846, the conditions seem very hard by today's standards but presumably were standard in the 1840s. Newcastle Barracks are described as being:

Built of brick and covered with slates. 9 rooms 43' x 27' x 8', each with 5 windows and 1 fireplace. 9 rooms 13' 6" x 12' 6" x 8' with 2 windows and 1 fireplace. 15 rooms 27' x 21' 6" x 11' 6"; 8 of these rooms have 3 windows and 1 fireplace each, and the other 7 rooms 2 windows and 1 fireplace each. The number of men, women and children usually occupying the barracks for the three years up to the return were: 530 men, 30 women, and 48 children. These barracks occupy 11 acres of ground, and within the boundary walls there are 6 wells, 4 of which are unfit for culinary purposes. There are also 3 rain-water tanks; viz., one to contain 32,000 gallons, one 18,000 gallons, and one 10,000 gallons. For the men there are 3 washing rooms; No. 1 for 208 men, No. 2 for 208 men, No 3 for 60 men. One wash house for the women containing 3 boilers. There were 3 cooking-houses; one with 18 boilers, one with 16 boilers and one with 12 boilers. [House of Commons Sessional Papers, 1847, Volume XXXVI.]

The Barrack Master at this time was Lieutenant J. Rutherford, late 94th Foot, (the Connaught Rangers 1881) who had taken the post on 1 October 1841, and whose salary was £182. 10s. 0d. per annum

Another event, which involved the 63rd Foot, (1st Battalion, the Manchester Regiment 1881) with the ever expanding railway system in the British Isles at that time, and which was watched by thousands of people, took place on 28 September 1849 when Her Majesty Queen Victoria opened the new High Level Bridge over the River Tyne, a great feat of civil engineering in Newcastle. Companies of The 63rd Foot, interspersed with dismounted volunteers of the Northumberland and Newcastle Volunteer Cavalry, lined the approaches to the bridge, and the Grenadier Company of the 63rd, with the Queen's Colour, mounted a Guard of Honour.

On 16 April 1851, Headquarters of the 21st Foot, (the Royal Scots Fusiliers 1881) moved from Edinburgh to Newcastle. According to the regimental records the battalion was located as follows: Newcastle Barracks 293 all ranks, Carlisle Castle 137 all ranks, Sunderland Barracks 204 all ranks, and Tynemouth Castle 134 all ranks. The battalion moved to Hull on 23 February 1852. During the time they served in the north five soldiers died of disease, three at Newcastle and two at Carlisle. However, regimental records do not always give the true facts. This is evident from the statement that three men died of disease in Newcastle. The fact is that one committed suicide, and an account of the tragic happening appeared in the *Newcastle Courant*, 6 February 1852:

Yesterday morning [Thursday 5th] a most determined act of suicide was committed at the Barracks, near this town, by a private in the 21st Royal North British Fusiliers named Joseph Slade. It appears the unfortunate deceased, who was hospital orderly, had for some time previous been labouring under considerable depression of mind, and had, on the morning of yesterday, unperceived, suddenly loaded his musket and shot himself through the head, the force of the charge completely carrying away the upper part of his skull, producing instantaneous death.

The opening of the High Level Bridge, 28 September 1849 as depicted by John Ventress in 'Royal Visits to Newcastle', 1851.

Eldon Square c.1841. This elegant development was, according to the historian McKenzie,
'one of the proudest moments of the taste and spirit of the Corporation in modern times'.

We have never been a militaristic nation and, except in times of war, we tend to ignore the armed services. But we do like pomp and circumstance; and whether it be on parade, or on a bandstand, a regimental band never fails to draw an appreciative audience. Thus it was that the bands of regiments from the barracks were always popular with the townspeople. A writer in the local press of 1841 reports that the band of the 61st Foot played at a cricket match between the military of Newcastle, Tynemouth and Sunderland, and the Northumberland team on Thursday 2 September 1841. The Northumberland team won with 16 runs to spare in one innings.

Two years later the *Newcastle Courant* reported: 'Lieutenant Colonel Bradshaw of the 37th Foot, (1st Battalion, the Hampshire Regiment 1881) now stationed in our barracks, with a laudable desire to afford the inhabitants of Newcastle a musical treat, has kindly ordered the excellent band of the regiment to play every Thursday afternoon (weather permitting) in Eldon Square.'

The practice of commanding officers to allow their regimental bands to play in Eldon Square on an afternoon during the season, and to play at the Lord Mayor's annual ball, became an accepted part of the social life of the town. Another aspect of the military involvement in the social life of Newcastle was that officers of the various regiments which were stationed in the barracks sponsored plays and other theatrical events in the Theatre Royal.

In 1854, when the 6th Inniskilling Dragoons were resident in the barracks, the public were admitted into the barracks on Sundays when the band played on the barrack-square. The public were also allowed into the barrack rooms and the canteen. This practice was later stopped; apparently the canteen was over-used! When the Dragoons left for the Crimea in 1854, via the High Level Bridge, an enthusiastic crowd turned out to see them off. A grateful pitman from Spital Tongues Colliery took the opportunity to present Mr Boat, the assistant surgeon of the regiment, with a gold headed whip as a mark of his appreciation for the recovery of his wife after the treatment he had given to her during the cholera epidemic of that year.

Military bands based in the barracks often played in Leazes Park, near the barracks, which opened in 1873. On Easter Monday and Tuesday, April 1884, the bands of the 5th Dragoon Guards and the 1st Newcastle Artillery Volunteers played in the morning and evening. When the recruits of the 4th (Militia) Battalion, the Durham Light Infantry, were doing their annual training in the barracks in June of that year, the band played in the park every afternoon from 3 to 4 p.m. In the following month the band of the Life Guards played during the annual flower show held in the park.

A great disaster occurred on 8 October 1854, during the fire that started on the premises of J. Wilson & Sons, worsted manufacturers, of Gateshead, and which eventually spread across the River Tyne to the Quayside of Newcastle. Among those helping to fight the fire on the Gateshead side of the River Tyne was a company of soldiers of the 26th Foot, (1st Battalion, the Cameronian Scottish Rifles 1881) under Ensign Camborne Hastings Paynter. He was killed along with Alexander Dobson, the son of John Dobson the Newcastle architect, and several other civilians, by being buried under tons of burning rubbish in Church Walk. There was great devastation on both sides of the river and such was the scale of the fire, '...the flames could be seen 50 miles away at Northallerton...' (*Fire Over the Tyne*, G. March) that extra troops had to be brought by rail from as far away as Carlisle, Tynemouth and Sunderland. Fire appliances were sent from Sunderland, Berwick, Hexham, Morpeth and Durham, and two

Ensign Paynter's grave can still be seen in Jesmond Old Cemetery, Newcastle, marked by a tombstone erected by his brother officers of the 26th Foot.

(Photo: J. Winter)

10	Companies
1	Lieutenant-Colonel
2	Majors
12	Captains
14	Lieutenants
10	Ensigns
1	Paymaster
1	Adjutant
1	Quarter-Master
1	Surgeon
2	Assistant-Surgeons
1	Sergeant-Major
1	Quarter-Master-Sergt
1	Paymaster-Sergeant
1	Armourer-Sergeant
1	Hospital Sergeant
1	Orderly-Room-Clerk
12	Colour-Sergeants
38	Sergeants
1	Drum-Major
24	Drummers
50	Corporals
950	Privates
1126	Total

floating fire fighting appliances came from Sunderland and Shields. The final damage was estimated to amount between £300,000 to £400,000; an enormous sum of money in those days.

As a result of a decision to increase the army by raising second battalions for certain regiments, Major and Brevet Lieutenant Colonel J.A. Vesey Kirkland, on the unpaid, unattached list, was directed by Horse Guards letter dated 26 October 1857, to proceed to Newcastle upon Tyne and there to raise a battalion 1,000 strong to be known as the 2nd Battalion, the Fifth (Northumberland) Fusiliers.[11] This battalion, originally raised during the Napoleonic Wars, had been disbanded in 1816. A War Office letter of 21 November 1857 directed the establishment of the battalion to be four depot and six service companies and to be recruited as shown left.

This was a typical infantry battalion of that period and by 25 December it had had been recruited to its establishment; it remained in Newcastle until 24 February 1858, when it was ordered to Aldershot. Letters and documents relating to the raising of the battalion, and correspondence with the Vicar of St Andrew's Church in Newgate Street, Newcastle upon Tyne, are held in the archives of the Royal Northumberland Fusiliers museum in Alnwick Castle.

A Parliamentary Committee had been set up in 1854 to report on barrack accommodation for the army. The report of this committee eventually led to major improvements in the conditions under which the soldiers lived. It proposed the setting up of separate quarters for married soldiers, separate dining rooms, dayrooms, ablution rooms and baths, laundry and drying rooms. It also recommended the removal of the urine tubs from the barracks and the erection of proper urinals with a water supply, and the replacement of cesspools by a drainage and sewerage system with an adequate water supply. Another return dated 18 June 1867, shows the barracks as accommodating seven officers and 174 cavalry soldiers, and 26 officers and 243 infantry soldiers.

As Newcastle Barracks had been originally erected to house cavalry and artillery, cavalry units were quartered in the barracks on a regular basis. According to the diary of Colour Sergeant Calladine, the troops or squadron usually changed in the Spring, and the historian of the Royal Dragoon Guards states that when cavalry regiments based in York were on the march to manoeuvres at Sheriffmuir, near Dunblane in

Scotland, the regiments always rested at Newcastle. One such regiment, the 14th Light Dragoons, arrived at Newcastle on 23 April 1867, and remained there until the end of August when they proceeded to Hamilton. During their stay they did excellent service at a fire rescue in the Central Exchange Buildings, on 4 August. Each man received a new uniform as a reward for his bravery and the damage done to his clothing. In addition each man was granted a gratuity of one week's pay.

Evidence of the fluctuations in recruiting for the army during this period can be found in *The History of the 2nd Battalion, the Northumberland Fusiliers.* A Horse Guards Memorandum of 31 May 1869 states that the minimum height for infantry recruits is reduced to 5 feet 6 inches. Then by General Order No. 8 of 1 February 1870, the height had been increased from 5 feet 6 inches to 5 feet 8 inches. This must have had a negative effect on recruiting as in another General Order, No. 59 of 4 June 1870, the height was once again reduced to 5 feet 6 inches. Even this was reduced to 5 feet 4½ inches by General Order No. 78 of 1876, then in General Order No. 60 1877, the minimum height went up again to 5 feet 5 inches, with an increase in the minimum chest measurement from 33 inches to 34 inches.

A poignant reminder of the consequences of disease and the epidemics which periodically affected Newcastle, and the unhygienic conditions in which soldiers and their families lived, can be seen in St Andrew's Church in Newgate Street, Newcastle. A marble memorial panel, sculpted by R. Beall of Newcastle, in commemoration of five men of 'G' Battery, 16 Brigade, Royal Artillery, who died in Newcastle Barracks between 1875 and 1877, was placed there by their comrades.

After a number of government enquiries resulting from an outcry by reformers after the serious mismanagement by the War Office of the Crimean War, it was found that over 250 barracks housing nearly 98,000 men had to be renovated. The work went on for many years. As part of the programme of rebuilding and renovation it was decided to extend Newcastle Barracks.[12]

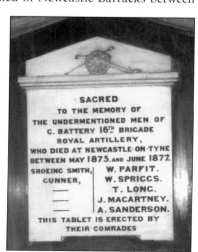

The memorial plaque to the five men of 'G' Battery, carved by R. Beall of Newcastle, on the south wall of St Andrew's Church. (Photo: T. Hewitson)

Following from this decision, at a Council meeting on Wednesday 18 February 1873, an application was made by the War Office to lease 6 acres to the south of the existing barracks at a rent of £5 per acre, upon which to build an infantry barracks. The Freemen of Newcastle had already agreed. At the Council meeting on Wednesday 4 March 1877, a Mr. Donkin moved the sealing of the lease to the Secretary of State for the War Department, for the barracks and ground adjoining as an extension, area 22 acres, 0 roods, 25 ¼ perches; rent £166. 4s. 0d., for a 99 year lease, (present site 11 acres). If the Council agreed to the lease the Secretary of State for War would surrender the present lease and a lease would be granted for the whole 22 ¼ acres at £7. 10s. 0d. per acre.[13]

This agreement caused a storm of protest in Newcastle, and at a Council meeting on Wednesday 12 March 1877, there was much public agitation about the proposed extension to the barracks in the direction of the Leazes, and the ratepayers were alarmed. A Mr. Rowell stated: '...any side is the best side which takes the barracks further from the town.' A month later, at a Council meeting held on 4 April 1877, a deputation was received opposing the extension of the barracks towards Leazes Park '...due to the type of people who frequented the barracks...' A petition against the extension signed by 1,000 people was presented to the Council.[14] History repeated itself in 1996 when Newcastle United Football Club's proposal to build a new football stadium on the very same Leazes caused great opposition, and a concerted attempt to try and stop it.

At a meeting on Wednesday 1 August 1877, a letter was read from the Royal Engineer office in Manchester, dated 17 May 1877, agreeing to move the extension from the south, to the north of the barracks. The Royal Engineers also stated that the War Office would not pay for the demolition of the Bull Park or the cottage attached, as the cost of removal would be £600. However, on 25 July 1877 the War Office agreed to meet this cost. The construction of the new extensions then proceeded.[15]

2

The 5th/68th Regimental Depots Established 1878-1898

Unfortunately, it has not been possible to find plans of the new extensions to the old barracks, nor has it been possible to find details of the dates on which the various buildings were constructed for the infantry barracks. To the north of the old artillery barracks a drill square was laid out which has been claimed to be the largest in the British Isles. A three story barrack block, 'U' Block, was built on the west side of the square to house the infantry soldiers, along with a cookhouse, dining rooms etc., to the rear of the block. An Institute Block was built on the north side of the square which housed a sergeants' mess, canteen, tailors shop, cobbler's and barber's shops. Married quarters 'W' Block, were built on the east side of the square facing the barrack block.

A new infantry officers' mess was still under construction on the south of the old barracks. Until it was ready the officers shared the Royal Artillery officers' mess and quarters. These quarters are now used as accommodation for students from Newcastle University and are the last of the old barrack blocks still standing apart from the remains of the former guardroom 'Q' Block, and the picquet room 'A' Block. These stood at the entrance to the original barracks, and were incorporated into the building of the public house originally named the Inn on the Park, later renamed the Cushy Billet. The construction of the new buildings to house the infantry, took in a road that went from Barrack Road to Spital Tongues, which meant that a public right of way had to be maintained through the barracks. This was to cause some controversy in later years with letters to the local press on the subject of bad language being used by drill instructors while civilians were walking through the barracks.

The original Georgian gatehouse of the barracks, constructed in 1806. (Photo: T. Hewitson)

Two Government reports published in 1871: *Report of the Army Sanitary Committee on Warming and Ventilation of Soldiers Barrack Rooms* and *Report of the Deputy Director of Works on Sanitary Appliances Introduced Into Barracks*, led to many improvements in the barracks. One of these would have been the construction of the seventy-bed hospital complex, 'G' Block, complete with mortuary and isolation block, built sometime between 1873 and 1877. This was situated in the old barracks area to the east of the Royal Artillery riding school, next to the present 'Sandhurst' Block. This hospital was demolished sometime in the 1970s and it is reputed to have been the last 'Florence Nightingale' pattern hospital in the United Kingdom.

Prior to 1878, depots of the infantry regiments were grouped into depot brigades, divisions and army corps. The 1st and 2nd Battalion depots of the 5th (Northumberland) Fusiliers were in 1 Brigade, 1 Division, 8 Army Corps, at Chatham, Kent. The 1st and 2nd Battalion depots of the 68th (Durham) Light Infantry were in 2 Brigade, 2 Division, 8 Army Corps, at Portland, Isle of Wight. In April 1878 it was decided to break up these depot brigades and establish Regimental Depots in their respective territorial areas; the 5th Fusiliers to Northumberland, and the 68th Light Infantry to Durham. The letter shown below was received by the 2nd Battalion, the 5th (Northumberland) Fusiliers, reference the formation of these new depots.

The following letter was received on 9th April, 1878, from the War Office, relative to formation and removal of Depot Companies. Details from *St George's Gazette*, December 1900:

Sir, – The Field Marshall Commanding in Chief, has been pleased to approve of the separation of the Depots from the Service Companies of the remaining Regiments in the Ist Army Corps, and of their movements to other Stations, I have the Honour by direction of His Royal Highness to request that you will be so good as to issue forthwith the necessary orders for the formation of the Depot 2nd Battalion, 5th Foot … and hold them in readiness to proceed to a station to be hereafter notified on receipt of a route from the Quarter-Master-General. Each Depot will consist of 2 Captains, (1 unmarried) 2 Subalterns, 2 Colour-Sergeants, 2 Sergeants and as limited number as possible of privates (to be selected from men pronounced physically fit for the Service without reference to length of Service) and report the number to this department, as well as the names of the Officers detailed. These detachment should be struck off the strength of Head-Quarters, on leaving, as they will be accounted for in separate returns from the Depot.

I have, &c.,

(Signed) R.H. Taylor, D.A.G.

In compliance with the above and in accordance with instructions contained in Horse Guards' minute, dated 6th April, 1878, and Horse Guards' Letter, dated 10th April 1878, $\frac{239\ 1/2}{22}$ the two Depot Companies left Chatham on 12th April 1878, by rail to Sheerness, to embark on H.M.S. Orantes for conveyance to Granton, thence by rail to Berwick-on Tweed, there to be stationed, the following being the strength of the Depot [see left].

On 29 July 1881, the depot companies of the Northumberland Fusiliers, (the 5th (Northumberland) Fusiliers pre 1881) transferred from Ravensdowne Barracks in Berwick, to establish the Regimental Depot in the new extension to Newcastle Barracks, in what was to be known as the 5th Regimental District. The Fusiliers were met on their arrival in the city by the band of the 1st Newcastle Rifle Volunteers who then played them into their new barracks.[1] This connection between the City of Newcastle and the depot of the Regiment was to continue until 1992, when the last representatives of the Regiment moved out of the barracks.

On 2 January 1884, the Depot Battery, Royal Artillery, left the barracks for Sunderland. They were replaced on 4 January by 'X' Battery which had sailed from Woolwich on the *Assistance*. The Regimental Depot of the Durham Light Infantry, (the 68th Foot pre 1881) under Colonel Niven, left the barracks in Sunderland and moved into Newcastle Barracks on 2 January 1884; with the permanent staff of the 4th (Militia) Battalion, the Durham Light Infantry, arriving on 10 January from Durham. The two regiments formed a joint depot to be designated as the 5th/68th Regimental District;[2] this joint depot lasted until 1939 when the Durham Light Infantry moved their depot to Brancepeth Castle, County Durham. However, the major units which administered the barracks and undertook garrison duties were usually from the Royal Artillery.

With the arrival of the depot of the Durham Light Infantry in the barracks, there was an increase in the number of troops in the Newcastle Garrison. To look after their spiritual needs a missionary named Amos Draper was appointed as an Army Scripture Reader to the troops, and in 1884 he moved into a house in Spital Tongues at the rear of the barracks.[3] His home was used for bible classes and tea meetings for soldiers and their wives. A Soldiers' Home in Hunter's Road, was officially opened by The Right Honourable Field Marshal Lord Roberts KP, GCB, GCSI, GCIE, VC at noon, on 5 May 1899, and he was presented with a silver key as a souvenir of the occasion.

1878, April 12th	
2 Companies	Officers
1 Captain	
2 Lieutenants	
Total 3	
4 Sergeants	Non-Com.-Officers and Men
5 Corporals	
1 Drummer	
28 Privates	
Total 38	
19 Women	
49 Children	
Remarks	
Captain Broad on passage home from India to join Depot.	
Names of Officers Captain E.J. Oldfield Lieutenant Hargrave Lieutenant Matthew	

The strength of the Berwick Depot in 1878.

Amos 'Daddy' Draper, who was appointed as an Army Scripture Reader to the troops in Newcastle Garrison in 1884. He lived firstly in Hunter's Road, where his house was used by soldiers in the barracks for bible classes and prayer meetings. When the Soldiers' Home was opened in 1899 he moved in as warden and lived there until 1922. The Home did not close until 1938.

(Photo: Miss B. Dobie)

It was reported that the Home was equipped with a billiard table, organ, piano, phonograph, that Sunday School, Sunday Evening Services and Temperance Meetings would be held, and that married families accommodation was available for those awaiting married quarters in the barracks. In October 1905, extensions to the Home were opened by Earl Grey, Governor General of Canada. 'Daddy' Draper, as he had by then become known to the troops, moved into the Home and ran it until 1922. The Home closed down in 1938 and it is now used as offices and book store by a Newcastle bookshop.

It was not until 1884 that the new mess was ready for the use of the officers of the 5th/68th depot. Due to the large number of recruits for the 3rd (Militia) Battalion, the Northumberland Fusiliers, in August 1884, tents had to be erected on the square to house them. Colour Sergeant Plowright, and Sergeants Shiel and Smith, were sent from the Militia Depot at Alnwick to help to train the militia recruits.

Such was the shortage of accommodation in the barracks at this period, that a large draft from the Durham Light Infantry depot left the barracks and sailed from

The Soldiers' Home in Hunter's Road was officially opened by Field Marshall the Right Honourable Lord Roberts KP, GCB, GCSI, GCIE, VC, at noon on 5 May 1899. The above photograph shows Lord Roberts and the official party being driven up Barrack Road, past Barrack Square, on the way to the opening ceremony.

The photograph below shows an excursion from the Home c.1910. (Photos: Miss B. Dobie)

Newcastle to London on the *Earl Percy*, then travelled by train to Portsmouth, where they boarded a troopship to join their regiment in Allahabad, India. On 6 November another draft from their depot left for the Durham Light Infantry battalion in Gibraltar; and a strong draft from the Royal Artillery also left the barracks. A draft of ninety from the Northumberland Fusiliers depot was sent to the 1st Battalion of the Regiment in Ship Street Barracks, Dublin, Ireland, on 1 November.

In his book *Newcastle Town*, 1885, R.J. Charlton describes the area in which the barracks had been built.

> After passing Barrack Square there are no more houses, and the Nun's Moor commences on the left – a narrow strip of grass at first but widening out as you proceed. Then on the right you pass the barracks, which stand upon the south-west corner of Castle Leazes, and after passing them the road has the Nun's Moor on either side, and so goes on westward in the direction of Ponteland.
>
> A truly rural scene after passing the squalor of the slum housing in Barrack Square, on the road up to the barracks.

Colonel Chester Master, late of the 5th (Northumberland) Fusiliers, presented the Fusilier officers of the depot with two marble topped tables which had been 'acquired' by men of the 1st Battalion of the Regiment at Lucknow, during the Indian Mutiny (1856-57). They arrived at Newcastle on 14 February 1885. These two tables can still be seen in the Fusilier Museum in Alnwick Castle, Northumberland.

On 1 April 1885, a detachment of volunteers comprising men from the Newcastle and Durham Engineers, Rifle and Artillery Volunteers, left from the barracks for service in the Egyptian campaign. In May it was reported that the number of soldiers in both depots numbered over 1,000 and that extra accommodation in the form of wooden huts was to be built on a grassed area outside the canteen block. In September, recruits of the 3rd (Militia) Battalion, the Northumberland Fusiliers, were housed in the new huts. A large draft from the Royal Artillery Depot sailed from Newcastle to Portsmouth on the SS *Assistance*, in October. It was also in this year that a large clock was placed over the canteen block and every alternate window in the long infantry barrack block was bricked up, probably to the relief of the soldiers occupying the block, as this would help to make the rooms warmer in the winter, and cooler in the summer.

5/68 REGIMENTAL DISTRICT BLOCK CANTEEN, COFFEE BAR AND LIBRARY

Bill of Fare:- Breakfast 3d. Dinner 6d. Tea 3d. Ham boiled, Fried Bacon and Eggs, Cheese, Spiced Beef, Tinned Beef, Liver and Bacon, Fish, Soup and Curries of sorts, and various other dishes at very low prices, and at all times of day.

An incident occurred in October 1886 that would create a sustained anti-racist discrimination campaign in the tabloid press if it were to happen today. A young man, 1582 Private Henry Annell, was recruited at Hounslow, London, for the Northumberland Fusiliers. On his arrival at Newcastle he was discovered to be '... a thorough Hindoo!...'. The officer commanding the depot at that time, not being disposed to accept any coloured men in the Regiment, reported the case to the War Office who ordered the recruit to be discharged for being wrongly enlisted.

His Royal Highness the Duke of Cambridge, Commander-in-Chief of the Army, visited Northumberland in 1887 and stayed at Cragside in Rothbury, Northumberland, the home of Lord Armstrong. On 13 May he arrived at the Central Station in Newcastle, by private train from Rothbury. He was met at the station by a Guard of Honour furnished by men from the Fusilier Depot, with the band of the 4th (Militia) Battalion, the Durham Light Infantry, and a mounted escort provided by the Northumberland (Hussars) Yeomanry. He then proceeded to open the Royal Jubilee Exhibition on the Town Moor. At 4 p.m. he reviewed 6,000 members of the North East Volunteer Battalions who paraded on the moor.

The annual treat for the children in the garrison was held on Friday 19 December 1890. A report in *St George's Gazette* gives a glowing account of the occasion:

The children assembled in the Garrison School at 3.30 pm., and they were marched to the Concert Room, R.A. Barracks, where they sat down to a remarkable good tea. Most of the ladies and officers in the Garrison assisted at the tables, and the pleasant remarks so often made by them, added much to the enjoyment of the children. After the repast, the room was cleared to prepare for an entertainment, which was arranged in real professional style, singing and conjuring adding greatly to the programme.

The greatest attraction during the evening was the distribution of the presents to the children. A full rigged ship, designed and built by Sergeant Pope, 4th D.L.I. (late of the "Old and Bold"), was erected on the stage, and from every rope and yard hung the many toys which were to be given to the children, the many and pleasing colours giving the ship a very gaudy aspect. The presents were handed to the children by Mrs Hope, who was ably assisted by Mrs Palmer, Major Whitehorne R.A., Lieut. Fletcher, Sgt-Major Kelly, Qmr-Sgt. Lusby, and many of the R.A. Staff-Sergeants.

The Officers' Mess of the Joint Infantry depot, 5th/68th Regimental District, Fenham Barracks, c.1899, demolished in 1938. The cannon and banners are from the Battle of Omdurman, 1898, in which the 1st Battalion, the Northumberland Fusiliers, took part.

Great credit is due to Mrs Hope and Mrs Palmer for their efforts to please the children, which were rewarded by the success of the whole affair, and the appreciation of the children and their parents. It is the wish of all that Colonel and Mrs Hope, may long be spared and remain among us to take part in the many treats to the children, as by their untiring efforts they have quite won the hearts of every soldier and family in the Garrison.

Soldiers from the two depots in the barracks combined their talents and formed a football team in 1892. They named the team the Newcastle Infantry Association Football Club and played a number of local teams such as: Green Market; Gateshead North Eastern Railway; Heaton North End and Walker Court; with varying degrees of success.

Sergeant J.J. Pitt of the depot training staff, a native of Bamburgh, Northumberland, who had joined the Northumberland Fusiliers at the barracks on 19 May 1887, was returning to Newcastle from London, on the SS *Londoner*, after conducting a draft to the 1st Battalion, the Northumberland Fusiliers. The ship was involved in a collision and sank off Grimsby on Sunday 14 May 1893. He was commended for his brave conduct during the sinking by Major General A.C. Wilkinson CB, commanding North East District, at a parade in Newcastle Barracks on 23 May 1893.[4]

His Royal Highness the Duke of York, arrived in Newcastle on Thursday, 5 April 1894, to officially open Rutherford College. On his departure from the Central Station

A lance-corporal from the barracks at the Town Moor Hoppings, c.1895.

to London in the evening, a Guard of Honour was provided by the 5th/68th Depots consisting of fifty men from the Northumberland Fusiliers and fifty men from the Durham Light Infantry, and the band of the 3rd Volunteer Battalion, the Northumberland Fusiliers

During the summer of 1893, the Northumberland Fusiliers was closed for recruiting, even in Northumberland, except for volunteers from the Militia Battalion. The reason given for this order in the *St George's Gazette* was that the Regiment, taken as a whole, was above its establishment, and that owing to the very large number of recruits enlisted in the preceding year, an enormous strain would occur when the time arrived for these men to be discharged into the reserve.

A great number of organised social and sporting events took place in Newcastle during the last years of the nineteenth century. In 1894 for instance, there was the Annual Temperance Festival on the Town Moor which had started after the racecourse had been removed to Gosforth Park in 1881, and in which the 63rd, 66th and 73rd Batteries, Royal Field Artillery based in the barracks, performed a musical ride. The Newcastle Tennis Week took place, and the Newcastle City Police sports were held at their sports ground in Jesmond. A great attraction at that event was the Regimental Band, and Pipes and Drums of the King's Own Scottish Borderers. Five thousand visitors attended the sports meeting during the course of the day.

Long service did not go unrecognised. At a social evening in the 5th/68th Depots sergeants' mess, a presentation of a canteen of cutlery, and a brooch for his wife, was made to Regimental Sergeant Major P. Murphy of the Light Infantry Depot who was retiring after thirty-seven years service in the Durham Light Infantry.

In 1898, with the return of the 2nd Battalion, the Northumberland Fusiliers from India to Portland, Isle of Wight, after sixteen years service overseas, it was decided to send a large party of officers and men to make a recruiting march through the County

Recruits and staff of the joint depots of the Northumberland Fusiliers and the Durham Light Infantry giving three cheers for the King's birthday in June 1929. They are parading in front of 'U' block in the infantry square.

In 1885 every alternate window had been bricked up, probably to make the rooms warmer in the winter. Evidence for the existence of the windows can be seen quite clearly on the facade of the building, in the middle row of windows by the central gable, where the outlines are clearly visible.

of Northumberland. Consequently 200 officers and men, with the battalion band and drums, arrived by special train at the Central Station, Newcastle, on Saturday evening 16 July. They were met by Colonel Upcher CB, DSO, commanding 5/68th Regimental District, and a party of officers from the 2nd Volunteer Battalion, the Northumberland Fusiliers. The band of the 3rd Volunteer Battalion, the Northumberland Fusiliers was also on hand to play the troops to the barracks. This was the first time that the battalion had been back in Newcastle in large numbers since it had been reformed there in 1857.

So great was the dense throng of people who had assembled to see the detachment arrive outside the Town Hall for an official greeting by the Lord Mayor of Newcastle, that mounted and foot police had to be used to clear the way for the marching soldiers. It was late into the evening before the tired and weary men arrived in the barracks. On the Sunday morning the detachment marched down Barrack Road for church parade at St Nicholas Cathedral, where once again thousands of people had turned out to see 'wor lads'.

On the Monday morning, 18 July, led this time by the band of the 2nd Volunteer Battalion, the Northumberland Fusiliers, which marched with them to Rosehill, Wallsend, the detachment set out on its march through Northumberland. This march eventually took them, with overnight stops, through Walker, Wallsend, Whitley Bay, Bedlington, Morpeth, Felton, Swarland, Alnwick, Whittingham, Rothbury, Kirkharle, Cambo, Wallington, Hexham, Prudhoe, Ryton, then back to Newcastle, where they arrived on Thursday 28 July, having been on the march ten days. Probably as a result of the recruiting march, 40 recruits enlisted in August, the highest monthly figure since 1892.[5]

Colonel Upcher relinquished command of the 5/68th Regimental District, and his place was taken by Colonel Garstin. In the artillery block, 14 battery was replaced by the newly arrived 86 Battery on 11 September. The Royal Engineers also started to build new stores for mobilisation equipment. Three hundred and twenty recruits passed through the Fusilier Depot in 1898, as opposed to only 172 in 1897. The total number of troops stationed within the barracks on 8 June 1899, in the two infantry depots, the three batteries of artillery and other troops was twenty-seven officers and 732 soldiers, plus wives and children. Each infantry depot had 40 permanent staff.

Newcastle Corporation gave Field Marshal Lord Wolesley, Commander-in-Chief of the Army, the Freedom of Newcastle on Saturday, 22 July 1899. After the presentation he reviewed the volunteer forces of Newcastle and Northumberland on the Town Moor. A combined force of 350 men from the Royal Artillery, and the two infantry depots from the barracks lined the parade ground for the review.[10] Six hundred and seven officers and men of the volunteers, with 481 horses and 54 guns marched past Lord Wolesley.

3 The South African War 1899-1902

On Monday 9 October 1899, men of the 1st Class Army Reserve of the Northumberland Fusiliers and the Durham Light Infantry, were called up due to the situation in South Africa. Between 12th and 18th October, 619 men reported to the Fusilier Depot and were sent on from there to the 2nd Battalion, the Northumberland Fusiliers at Portsmouth. Recruiting was brisk and once again shortage of accommodation in the barracks began to cause problems.

Mobilisation of the 7th Division Ammunition Column, the Royal Artillery, took place in the barracks at the beginning of January 1900. When the column left, their barrack space was occupied by Imperial Yeomanry volunteers from the Northumberland (Hussars) Yeomanry. One of those who volunteered for the Yeomanry was Karl Spurgin, whose account reflects vividly the attitudes and sentiments of the young men of that era.

About Christmas-time 1899, when reverses were being met with on every side, while Ladysmith, Kimberly and Mafeking were still in a state of siege, a cry went up for more men, mounted if possible, to assist our gallant army in South Africa, which was striving hard for supremacy. Undoubtedly our country had reached a crisis; we must conquer or go under – which should it be?

Attention was turned to the Yeomanry, men who could ride well and shoot straight. Plenty of such men were to be had for the asking; young fellows, sportsmen to the core, sons of professional men, farmers, merchants, fellows in all stations of life with the true British love of sport strong in them. The proposal originated in the Counties of Northumberland and Durham, and was taken up at once by patriotic gentlemen, who forwarded the scheme with heart and soul.

Sincere thanks are due to Mr. H. H. Scott, of Hipsburn, Northumberland, as the originator of the Northumberland and Durham Counties Imperial Yeomanry, who headed the list for the Yeomanry fund with £1,000. His son was one of the first to volunteer. Mr. Scott informed Earl Grey of his scheme, and the result was that a telegram was forwarded to the Secretary of State for War saying that Northumberland would provide a well-equipped corps of one hundred mounted infantry. Several telegrams were despatched at the same time to various gentlemen asking them if they would follow the example of Mr. Scott. Before the evening of the same day £10,000 was subscribed. The total fund raised in the two counties ultimately reached £50,085, towards which Northumberland contributed £33,558, and Durham £16,527 – the largest sum raised by any fund in the country.

The offer was accepted by the Secretary of State for War, and a following proclamation was issued by the Government practically asking the nation to follow the example of Northumberland. This undoubtedly had a most welcome effect on the Yeomanry movement. Then Colonel Cookson[1] took the matter in hand, and instead of the original one hundred, a force of 355 mounted men was raised, which was afterwards known as A, B and C Squadrons, or 14th, 15th, and 55th Squadrons, and sent to the front.

Candidates applied at the Yeomanry headquarters in Northumberland Road, Newcastle upon Tyne, where they were medically inspected, the test being very severe. Many men were rejected for poor sight, though the majority were fine athletic fellows, apparently fit for any amount of hard work. Next came the riding and shoot-

A member of the Northumberland and Durham Imperial Yeomanry training at the Barracks just before going overseas to South Africa. (Photo: R. Thompson)

ing tests; the former was not very severe, though a few men were rejected on this score. A still further thinning occurred over the shooting test, although every chance was given [to] a man who was any marksman at all.

Those who had proved themselves so far efficient were sent up to the Artillery Barracks, Barrack Road, where they got their first taste of military discipline, and were drilled daily, both mounted and on foot. Horses speedily arrived, being purchased under the supervision of Mr. Elphick,[2] veterinary surgeon. The average height of of the mounts would be about 14.2. [hands] and a good hardy sample. Some of the men brought their own chargers, being allowed £40 by the Government for them. Men entered with spirit into the work before them, grooming their horses, cleaning up saddlery, kit, drilling and getting gradually more military looking, though they never quite aspired to being cavalrymen – they were too much like the fox-hunting fraternity. Eagerly they awaited the naming of the date on which they were really to make a start for the front, and at last the long-wished-for news came; they were to entrain on February 1st, 1900.

Before our departure from Newcastle a most impressive service was held in the Cathedral [St Nicholas']; the whole function was most earnest and touching, and went a long way towards cheering us up, giving us hope and courage to face the trials and dangers that must inevitably be met with on active service.

The morning of February 1st broke dull and cold, with snow lying thick on the ground.

Through this we trudged to the Grand Assembly Rooms, Barras Bridge, (Haymarket) where a farewell breakfast was given. In the evening at 6.30, we paraded at the Barracks, drew our rifles from the stores, packing them in cabs, placed bridles on our horses, carefully sheeted them, and in double file marched off to the Central Station. The horses were very fresh, and rather objected to the crowds that lined the streets to witness our departure. On arriving at the station we placed the horses in cattle-trucks, heads all one way, and tied up very short; after a little trouble and exertion they were soon all safely aboard. The men then entrained, the crowd being most enthusiastic. Our feelings can be better imagined than described; although we endeavoured to keep a bold front, somehow a troublesome lump would keep rising in the throat as we shook hands for the last time for many a long day with friends and relations who had come to see us depart.[3]

At the same time three Special Service Companies of infantry were being formed in the barracks, two from the Volunteer Battalions of the Northumberland Fusiliers, and one from the Volunteer Battalions of the Durham Light Infantry. These companies left the barracks on 10 January 1900. They eventually sailed for South Africa on 22 February, arriving in Cape Town on 17 March. Among those who volunteered was Sergeant George Middlemiss, from Glanton, Northumberland, a member of 'D' Company, 1st Volunteer Battalion, the Northumberland Fusiliers. He was held back as he was a married man and at the age limit. However, he was ordered to report to the barracks on 26 March where he was medically examined and approved, transferred to the First Class Army Reserve, then sent back home to await call up.

Shortly after this he was called back to the barracks and after a spell of training his party was sent to Strensall Barracks near York, where he arrived on Saturday, 5 April. At midnight on Thursday, 10 April 1900, his draft and drafts from the volunteer battalions of the East Yorkshire Regiment; the West Yorkshire Regiment; the Lincolnshire Regiment and the Durham Light Infantry; left Strensall Station for London, where they embarked on the P&O ship *Assaye* on which they sailed for South Africa the following day.[4]

Among the depot staff dealing with the recall of reservists and the training of volunteers for South Africa was Regimental Sergeant Major John Fraser, who had been posted to the depot of the Northumberland Fusiliers in January 1899 after serving nearly twenty-two years with the 2nd Battalion of the Regiment. In March 1900, a draft of militiamen from the Prince of Wales Leinster Regiment and the Royal Munster Fusiliers, who were to be part of a draft of 200 for the 2nd Battalion, the Northumberland Fusiliers in South Africa, arrived in the barracks. When the draft was marched to the Central Station, on the evening of 23 April 1900, Sergeant Major Fraser discovered that a Private Docherty of the Royal Munster Fusiliers was absent so he replaced Docherty with a substitute.

He had the draft aboard the train when he heard the provost-sergeant shouting from the footbridge in the station that he had Private Docherty, who was obviously the worse for drink. As the train was about to leave Fraser pulled out the substitute and tried to push Docherty into the compartment. Docherty would have none of this:

"Not in there sorr! … Ye see sorr, I want Doyle – Paddy Doyle sorr-ye'll be knowin him? … Are ye there Doyle? Are ye there Paddy me bhoy?…" But Doyle was not, so Docherty ran down the platform shouting. "Sure, 'tis Paddy Doyle I'm wanting … Are ye there, Paddy?…Doyle! Doyle!" He found Doyle in the last carriage. Then with a wild shout of: "Hiven be praised, Oi've found ye at last, Paddy!" he scrambled into the compartment.

The event had a sad sequel; both Docherty and Doyle died in South Africa.[5]

Two extra regular battalions were sanctioned for the Northumberland Fusiliers on 12 February 1900, to be designated as the 3rd and 4th Battalions.[6] The 3rd (Militia) Battalion was accordingly renumbered as the 5th (Militia) Battalion, the Northumberland Fusiliers. Having volunteered for overseas service the Militia

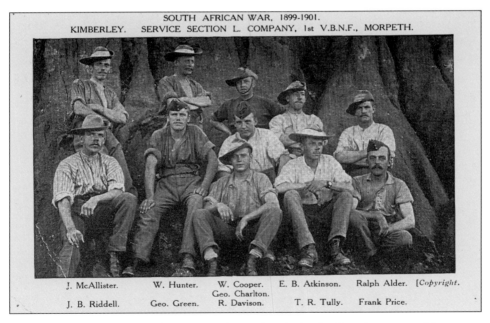

SOUTH AFRICAN WAR, 1899-1901.
KIMBERLEY.   SERVICE SECTION L. COMPANY, 1st V.B.N.F., MORPETH.

J. McAllister.	W. Hunter.	W. Cooper.	E. B. Atkinson.	Ralph Alder.	[Copyright.
		Geo. Charlton.			
J. B. Riddell.	Geo. Green.	R. Davison.	T. R. Tully.	Frank Price.	

All the men shown here were from Morpeth, Northumberland. When they returned from South Africa they were installed as Freemen of Morpeth. On the extreme left of the back row is J. McAllister who eventually became Company Sergeant Major of the company which was redesignated as 'A' Company, 7th Battalion the Northumberland Fusiliers (TF), after the Haldane reforms of 1908. He was present with the Comrades' Association, at the presentation of new Colours to the 7th Battalion in Alnwick Castle on 8 September 1961.
The Service Companies were organised, equipped and trained in the Barracks before going to South Africa. (Photo: T. Hewitson)

Battalion was serving in Malta. Pressure on the depot to supply recruits increased. From September 1899 to March 1900, 432 recruits and 274 volunteers passed through the Fusilier Depot. A draft of 200 Militia Reservists was kitted out and posted to South Africa on 24 April, and 400 Royal Reservists were sent to the Royal Northern Reserve Regiment at Aldershot. Quartermaster Sergeant J.T. Rowlands, who had spent ten years at the Fusilier Depot, was posted to the newly raised 3rd Battalion, the Northumberland Fusiliers at York.

By November recruiting had fallen off. Bandmaster Wallace and the bandboys of the 2nd Battalion, the Northumberland Fusiliers, who had been left behind when the battalion sailed for South Africa, were posted to the barracks. It was hoped that the band would stimulate recruiting on the regular Sunday morning church parades down Barrack Road and Gallowgate. By this time wounded and sick men were returning to the barracks from South Africa. On 4 December 1900, the 4th (Militia) Battalion, the Durham Light Infantry, arrived at the barracks for disembodiment. The band from the depot had played them from the Central Station.

Following the death of Her Royal Highness Queen Victoria, the proclamation of His Majesty King Edward VII took place in Newcastle on 25 January 1901. Troops from 24 Brigade, Royal Field Artillery, Regimental Depot, the Northumberland Fusiliers, and Regimental Depot, the Durham Light Infantry, under the command of Colonel C.S. Gordon CB, all based in Newcastle Barracks, lined St Nicholas Square where the proclamation was read by the Town Clerk.

This photograph from **Northern Gossip**, *a local magazine, 27 July 1901, shows the Elswick Battery in Barrack Road on their way to the Cathedral. The Barracks can be seen to the rear.*

In January 1901, 70 recruits joined the Fusiliers and 60 were sent to the 4th Battalion, the Northumberland Fusiliers, on the 21st. Recruiting for the third and fourth Fusilier Volunteer Service Companies was started. By February two officers, one warrant officer, three sergeants and 30 privates had volunteered. In the same month 120 recruits left the depot of the Fusiliers. The two Volunteer Companies left Newcastle on a special train on 14 March. They were played to the Central Station by the bands of 2nd Battalion, the Northumberland Fusiliers, and the 2nd and 3rd (Volunteer) Battalions, the Northumberland Fusiliers. A large number of Mounted Police had to be used to clear the way through the enormous crowds which lined the route to the station. Bandmaster Ivermee of the 1st Battalion, the Northumberland Fusiliers, with 15 bandboys, arrived in Newcastle on 19 March to be attached to the Regimental Depot while his battalion was in South Africa.

The first and second Fusilier Volunteer Service Companies arrived back in Newcastle, from South Africa, at 7 a.m. on 21 May 1901. They were met at the Central Station by the Mayor and Corporation and played up to the barracks by the bands of the 2nd Battalion, the Northumberland Fusiliers, and the 2nd and 3rd (Volunteer) Battalions, the Northumberland Fusiliers. By 1.30 p.m. the 200 men had been demobilised and were on their way home.

During June, 110 men of the Imperial Yeomanry were demobilised from the barracks. The annual Newcastle Race Week Temperance Festival took place and attracted

The return of the Durhams, as they pass St Nicholas' Cathedral. This photograph is from **Northern Gossip**, *15 June, 1901.*

thousands of visitors; the band of the 2nd Battalion, the Northumberland Fusiliers, played during the three days of the Festival.

Colonel A.L. Woodland CB took command of the 5th/68th Regimental District in July.

A Thanksgiving Service was held in St Nicholas Cathedral on Saturday 10 August to celebrate the return of the men of the Imperial Yeomanry and Volunteer Service Companies, followed by a banquet in Olympia. The Newcastle members of these units received the Freedom of the City.

January 1902 saw a fifth Volunteer Service Company being raised for the Northumberland Fusiliers. However, enthusiasm seemed to have waned; only two officers and 54 other ranks had volunteered when recruiting was stopped. From the start of recruiting to the end, the 1st, 2nd, and 3rd (Volunteer) Battalions of the Northumberland Fusiliers, had provided 674 officers and soldiers for service with the two regular battalions in South Africa.

Among those who enlisted at this time was a young man from Oxhill, County Durham. His widowed father had remarried and the young Robert Wearmouth was having domestic difficulties with his step-mother. He ran away from home and made his way to Newcastle Barracks where he joined the Northumberland Fusiliers. He very soon regretted his decision.

> ... Recruits drill continued for seven months, with several parades a day, apart from Sunday, including a severe gymnastic course. Day by day and week after week we repeated a hundred times our various exercises. As a unit of about thirty recruits we had to learn how to shoulder arms, present arms, trail arms, down arms, until we could do anything with a rifle except shoot straight. We were taught to walk smartly with head erect and chest out. In short we had to be like a walking automaton, with never a word why all this. It had to be done no matter why. 'Ours not to reason why' ...[6]

After his recruit training which took place in Newcastle and Whitley Bay, he was posted to the 3rd Battalion, the Northumberland Fusiliers based at Portland, Isle of Wight. He later served on the Island of Antigua, then South Africa. After he left the army, he entered the Methodist Ministry and eventually became the Reverend R.F. Wearmouth MA, BSc, PhD, FMH, HCF. He served as an Army Chaplain during the 1914-18 War, and in the 1950s was living in Cullercoats, North Tyneside.

The first issue of the new 1902 pattern khaki service dress was made to the depot staffs in May, and in the same month the second and third Volunteer Service Companies arrived back in Newcastle; 1st Battalion Company on 5 May, and the 2nd Battalion Company on 22 May. Sergeant Major Wooll and 11 soldiers from the 1st Battalion, the Northumberland Fusiliers, arrived at the depot on 29 May, bound for the Coronation of His Majesty King Edward VII.

The Haymarket, Newcastle upon Tyne, 4p.m. Monday 22 June 1908.

The Northumberland War Memorial for the South African War of 1899 to 1902 is unveiled. The entire depots of the Northumberland Fusiliers and the Durham Light Infantry, with a detach-ment from 8 Brigade, the Royal Field Artillery, based in the Barracks, with the corps of Drums and 150 of the 2nd Battalion, the Northumberland Fusiliers took part in the ceremony.

(See also page 54)

(Photo: T. Hewitson)

South African War Medals were presented to members of the depot staff of the Northumberland Fusiliers on 27 August, and the process of demobilisation started. Three drafts of 100 each arrived at the Fusilier Depot during August, and another draft of 100 was expected on 31 August.

Captain Burdon, a Militia officer of the 5th Battalion, a member of the Northumberland coal owning family who lived in Hartford Hall, near Bedlington, Northumberland, and who had been doing duty at the Fusilier depot since 1899, was discharged. Bandmasters Ivermee and Wallace, with the their bandboys, left the depot to embark on the SS *Plassey* on 16 April for South Africa. The orders for the 2nd Battalion band were cancelled as the battalion was to return to England.

All details from the 2nd Battalion left the depot on 4 February 1903 for Gravesend to await the arrival of the battalion from South Africa. On 1 March, the last batch of time expired men from South Africa arrived at the depot. After that all those return-ing were dealt with at the Discharge Centre at Gosport. From November 1900, 2,500 men had been discharged or transferred to the Reserve from the depot, in addition to 250 men of the Yeomanry.

4 Peacetime Soldiering Again
1903-1914

In January 1903, two drafts of 103 each were sent from the barracks to the 4th Battalion, the Northumberland Fusiliers, in Dublin. On 5 February, Sergeant A. Carter, the officers' mess sergeant left the army after 29 years service with a pension of 2s. 6d (12 $\frac{1}{2}$p) per day. In February 1903, the 'Broderick' cap was taken into wear by non-commissioned officers and soldiers in the barracks. This was a peakless cap, similar to the cap worn by sailors of the Royal Navy, and was, perhaps, the most unpopular headdress ever introduced into the British Army.

Detachments from both the Northumberland Fusiliers, and the Durham Light Infantry Depots, attended a Memorial Service in St Mary's Church, Gateshead, for the unveiling of a tablet by Colonel M.H. Lambert, Commanding Officer of the 4th (Militia) Battalion, the Durham Light Infantry, in memory of the Durham Light Infantry men who had died in South Africa. Four of them had died while serving with the 2nd Battalion, the Northumberland Fusiliers.

Second Lieutenants Jackson and Boyle, with Sergeant Major Buckthought, Lance Sergeants' Sleath and Burnell, arrived at the Fusilier Depot on 20 May to retrieve the Colours of the 2nd Battalion, the Northumberland Fusiliers, which had been lodged there during the South African War. Field Marshal Lord Roberts, the Commander-in-Chief, inspected the combined depots on parade on 24 June. He also inspected the Institute building, married quarters, and the Soldiers' Home in Hunter's Road, lunching in the officers mess afterwards.

During July and August 1903, 169 recruits were sent to the home battalions of the Northumberland

Lord Roberts in full dress uniform, wearing his orders and decorations. (Photo: T. Hewitson)

Fusiliers; 150 to the 2nd Battalion at Gravesend, and 19 to the 4th Battalion in the Royal Barracks, Dublin. At the North East District Rifle Meeting at Strensall, near York, on 20/21 August, a team from the depot of the Durham Light Infantry, won the Championship Cup and Strensall Cup.

The strength of the Northumberland Fusiliers on 1 January 1904, was as follows:
1st Battalion: 762 all ranks.   Mauritius.
2nd Battalion: 629 all ranks.   Gravesend.
3rd Battalion: 703 all ranks.   South Africa.
4th Battalion: 687 all ranks.   Dublin.
Depot: 157 all ranks.   Newcastle.
Total: 2,938 all ranks.

By February this number had increased to 3,100. This figure did not include the three volunteer battalions of the Regiment. Owing to the strength of the Regiment recruiting was halted for it everywhere in the British Isles except Northumberland. Such had been the influx of recruits in the early part of 1904 that accommodation again became a problem. It was so bad that recruits were issued with their uniforms and equipment then sent directly to their respective home battalions for training.

A notice appeared in the *St George's Gazette* for January, warning of a man calling himself J.L. Lesley, who was claiming to have served with the Northumberland Fusiliers in South Africa, and that he had been discharged from the military hospital at Netley two years previously. He had obtained board and lodging and borrowed sums of money under false pretences.

The Channel Fleet march along Collingwood Street, Newcastle, on 27th September 1904.

On 24 June, the official birthday of His Majesty King Edward VII, the combined depots paraded in review order (full dress) at noon. The royal salute was given, followed by three cheers for the King. The rest of the day was declared a holiday; which was very probably of much more interest to the recruits than a birthday parade.

In August the Fusilier depot went into a tented camp at Whitley Bay (now the site of the Hartley Caravan Park) to fire the annual range course. There was a problem with this rifle range as a right of way ran across the middle. This caused the firing point officer much frustration because of the constant stream of carts, carriages, bicycles, walkers, and other curious persons who had: 'cum te waatch the sowljers!'

During the last week of September, the Channel Fleet, under the command of Lord Charles Beresford, paid a visit to the Tyne. There were numerous banquets, dinners, lunches, dances and other social events laid on the for the officers and men of the Royal Navy. On Thursday 27 September, sailors from the Fleet marched through Newcastle (see photograph on page 49). Recruits from the combined depots and other units lined the route in some of the principal streets.

Recruiting was opened again in all the English districts in January 1905, and 120 recruits enlisted in the Fusilier Depot. In March, a party from the barracks went to the Elswick Works, on the River Tyne, to see the launching of the battleship *Kashima* for the Japanese navy. One hundred Fusilier recruits were sent to the 4th Battalion at Limerick, Ireland.

Permanent staff of the 3rd Battalion Northumberland Fusiliers (Special Reserve). The headquarters of the Special Reserve Battalion had been moved from Alnwick to the barracks after the Haldane reforms of 1908. Standing outside the 5th/68th Officers' Mess in the barracks are Colour Sergeant Cooper holding the King's and Regimental Colour of the battalion. The escorts from left to right are Sergeant Maynard, Sergeant Ouzman and Sergeant Richardson.
(Photo: T. Hewitson)

Major Byrne, Depot Quartermaster, the Durham Light Infantry, retired in May 1905 after forty years service, the last twelve of which he had spent in the barracks. All the officers of the joint depots subscribed to a silver salver engraved with the two regimental crests and replicas of their signatures, with which he was presented when he left.

A detachment from each unit in the barracks, commanded by Captain Wake of the Durham Light Infantry, paraded in November 1905, for the unveiling of the South African War Memorial at Gateshead. A site in Haymarket Square in Newcastle, occupied by a three cornered cabmen's shelter, was designated as the site on which the Northumberland South African War Memorial would be built.

Colonel Ovans CB, took over command of the 5/68th Regimental District from Colonel Woodward CB, in April 1906.

In June 1906, His Majesty King Edward VII, and Her Majesty Queen Alexandra, stayed at Alnwick Castle as guests of the Duke and Duchess of Northumberland. On Wednesday 1 July 1906, they visited Newcastle. The city streets were decorated with flags and bunting. All the tram posts were painted and stands were erected in various places for spectators. Arriving at the Central Station at 11 a.m. the royal party was met by a Guard of Honour mounted by men of the Northumberland Fusiliers from the barracks. Unfortunately, the Durham Light Infantry Depot could not muster enough

Troops in tented accommodation on the artillery square, c.1908. They are probably doing their militia training. The artillery riding school is situated on the left, and the large building behind it, centre rear, was the hospital block. Note the water point, at the lower edge of the photograph, which was probably formed from one of the original six wells.

(Photo: T. Hewitson)

A Brigade of Royal Field Artillery, very likely 35 Brigade, which consisted of 27, 36 and 60 Batteries, returning to the barracks via Hunter's Road. They had perhaps been taking part in some sort of ceremony as full dress was only worn on special occasions. Full dress was phased out after World War I, except for certain units. (Photo: Miss B. Dobie)

men to mount a guard. The route of the procession through the city was lined by 3,000 regular and volunteer soldiers. Children of the married soldiers living in the barracks were taken in artillery wagons to a spot near Grey's Monument. They had all been given small Union flags to wave as the royal party went by. The King unveiled a statue of Queen Victoria at the Royal Victoria Infirmary, and after a luncheon in the Assembly Rooms, His Majesty knighted the Lord Mayor of Newcastle.

Newcastle Barracks were very quiet in the month of June, the reason being that 30 Brigade, Royal Field Artillery, had left for Trawsfynnyd, North Wales, for their annual gunnery practice shoots.

In October the silver and pictures of the 4th Battalion, the Northumberland Fusiliers, were sent from Ireland to the officers' mess of the 5/68th Depot, and in November the rear party of the now disbanded 4th Battalion arrived at the barracks to hand over the battalion documents to the record office. The 4th Battalion was finally disbanded at 12 p.m. on Saturday 26 January 1907. The 3rd Battalion, the Northumberland Fusiliers, was disbanded from the ship on which it arrived from South Africa on 4 March 1907.

Anticipating the Haldane reforms which were to be initiated in April 1908, recruit-

The scene in St Nicholas Square, Newcastle, just before noon on 11 March 1914. A detachment of three officers and fifty men, and the Corps of Drums, from the 1st Battalion, the Northumberland Fusiliers, under the command of Captain E.B. Gordon, had come to Newcastle Barracks, from Cambridge Barracks in Portsmouth, to lay up the old Colours of the battalion, which had been presented in 1864, in St Nicholas Cathedral. The cadets in khaki are from Dame Allen's School. (Photo: T. Hewitson)

ing began for the 3rd (Special Reserve) Battalion, the Northumberland Fusiliers. This was the former Militia Battalion which had its headquarters at Alnwick. As part of the reforms it was now to be based in the barracks and designated as a Special Reserve Battalion with new conditions of service. With the disbanding of the 3rd and 4th Battalions, the Militia Battalion had resumed its original designation as the 3rd Battalion. Royal Engineers started to refurbish the old record offices in the barracks in March ready for their occupation by the newly formed headquarters of the Northumbrian Division of the Territorial Force, also formed as a result of the Haldane reforms.[1] As a further result of the reforms, 8 Brigade, the Royal Field Artillery, stationed in the barracks, was reorganised as a training brigade, reduced to forty horses, and started training artillery special reservists for six months in the basics of drill and semaphore.

Two major events took place in Newcastle on Monday, 22 June 1908. At 2.45 p.m. the King's and Regimental Colours of the 3rd and 4th Battalions, the Northumberland Fusiliers, were laid up in St Nicholas Cathedral. A detachment of 6 officers and 150 men from the 2nd Battalion, the Northumberland Fusiliers, accompanied by the recruits and staff of the Regimental Depot led by the Corps of Drums of the 2nd Battalion, marched from the barracks to the cathedral with the Colours.

After the ceremony of laying up the Colours, the detachment marched through enormous crowds up Northumberland Street to the Haymarket, where at 4 p.m. the Northumberland War Memorial for the South African War was unveiled by Lieutenant General Sir Laurence Oliphant KCVO, KCB, Commander-in-Chief Northern Command. The memorial, which stands in the Haymarket, was built with stone from Cragside, Northumberland, by Mr. J.C. Ferguson of Newcastle, and the winged angel on top of the memorial was sculpted by Mr. Macklin who had designed it. The winged figure was cast in bronze, in France. All the units named on the memorial were represented and the entire Regimental Depot of the Durham Light Infantry took part in the ceremony, as did a detachment of the Royal Field Artillery based in the barracks.[2]

In July the band of the 2nd Battalion, the Durham Light Infantry, was based in the Light Infantry Depot in the barracks while carrying out a series of engagements in Newcastle.

The Quartermaster General, and the Master General of Ordnance, inspected the barracks on 22 January 1909. It was believed that the Headquarters of the 4th Battalion, the Durham Light Infantry, (Special Reserve) was to be transferred to Barnard Castle.

A great improvement was made to the look of the barracks in the autumn of 1911, when men of the Royal Field Artillery based in the barracks started planting trees around the square and married quarters, and an avenue of trees at the back of the officers quarters. Lieutenant-General Sir H. Plumer KCB, the new Commander-in-Chief of Northern Command, inspected the barracks on 24 November, and Major-General Sir Charles Ferguson, Inspector of Infantry, visited the combined depots on 19 December 1911.

Hartley Rifle Range, near Whitley Bay, Northumberland, which had been used by the troops from Newcastle Barracks and the local volunteer units since 1881, was reported to be closing in August 1912, and rifle shooting was to take place at the newly built rifle range at Berwick Hill, near Ponteland, Northumberland. This rifle range is still in use today.

A party of two officers and sixty men of the 1st Battalion, the Northumberland Fusiliers, plus their Corps of Drums, brought the old Colours of the battalion from Portsmouth to Newcastle. At an impressive ceremony in St Nicholas Cathedral on 11 March 1914, the Colours were laid up. The detachment from the 1st Battalion had escorted the Colours from the barracks to the cathedral, where recruits from the depot lined St Nicholas Square. Over 2,000 people attended the laying up of the Colours in the cathedral.[3]

5   The Great War 1914-1919

Great Britain finally declared war against Germany on 4 August 1914. Preparations for mobilisation had begun on 28 July 1914, when men from the depot were sent to guard oil tanks in the district. 1,776 reservists of the Northumberland Fusiliers were recalled to the barracks in Newcastle. Within forty-eight hours all except forty-four had reported. A draft of 600 was sent immediately to the 1st Battalion, the Northumberland Fusiliers at Portsmouth, and from there the battalion landed in France with the Expeditionary Force on 13 August.

This was a chaotic period for the staffs of the two infantry depots, the Royal Artillery, and other units in the barracks. Such was the influx of recruits in the early days of August and September that it was virtually impossible to deal with them. The barracks were swamped with men. About 1,000 men were in civilian billets in the city. At one stage there were 4,650 men in the barracks.

It was just as well that the War Office had pre-war married quarters for married soldiers, and other property in Newcastle Garrison. The married quarters were in Abbotsford Terrace, Ancrum Street, Croydon Road, Leazes Gate Villa, Shuttleworth Street and Wingrove Avenue. Bellegrove Terrace accommodated Royal Engineer offices.

Due to the unprecedented numbers of recruits arriving at the barracks in 1914, battalions of 1,100 were formed and despatched to various parts of the country. This photograph shows members of the 10th (Service) Battalion, Northumberland Fusiliers in October 1914 wearing the navy blue uniform issued to Kitchener's battalions because of the shortage of khaki cloth.
(Photo: T. Hewitson)

There were also seventeen married quarters in Tynemouth. A great number of houses and other buildings of various types were requisitioned during the war. For a full list of these properties readers may refer to *List of Lands and Buildings in the Occupation of the War Department, 1 June 1918 (Northern Command)*, printed for the Lands and Buildings Reconstruction Committee.

Evidence of the chaos during this period can be found in a report in the local press of September 1914. Thomas Sewell, a thirty-year-old Gateshead man, was charged with: 'Gaming in a Public Place', and 'dishonestly acquiring food to the value of 10/- [fifty pence] at His Majesty's expense.' It appears that he had been going into the barracks in the morning and running a penny 'Crown & Anchor' board (a gambling game) falling in with the recruits for his meals, then going home at night.[1]

An early volunteer who was caught up in the excitement of the times was George Beatty, of Pancake Row, Sheepwash, Northumberland. He had gone to the drill hall in Ashington to volunteer for the Royal Navy, unfortunately he could not meet the medical requirements. When he got back home his brother Ned told him that he had joined the Northumberland Fusiliers. George went immediately to the police station in Bedlington, and volunteered for the same regiment:

Ned and me reported to Newcastle Barracks where we were given a blanket and put into a barrack room. As we were pit lads, and always used to plenty of big hot dinners, by tea time we were very hungry. A Lance Corporal, who seemed a nice man, came into the room and we asked him when we would get something to eat. He took us to the cookhouse where we were given a lump of cheese, half a fadge (a round flat loaf of bread) and a tin bowl of tea. When I asked him if this was all we were going to get? He said: 'Lad! there will plenty of times when if you get this meal you will think yourselves bloody lucky! ... so bugger off!'[2]

Not only young men volunteered. An old soldier, ex-Sergeant W.F. Horn, who had been discharged to pension on medical grounds in February 1914, was one of the first through the barrack gates. He had enlisted into the Northumberland Fusiliers in 1894 and served with the 1st Battalion at the Battle of Omdurman (Sudan) in 1898, right through the South African War of 1899-1902, then in Mauritius and India. He failed his medical examination, but as he was so keen to serve he was appointed as recruiting sergeant at North Shields.

He did not live to see the end of the war as he died in November 1917.[3]

When General Plumer visited the barracks on 6 September 1914, there were 3,500 men on parade with another 500 out route marching. From 1 September to 31 December 1914, 15,570 recruits passed through the depot.

The barracks was neither built, nor staffed, to deal with such huge numbers of recruits. the Northumberland Fusilier Depot only had a staff of three officers and about a dozen NCOs, so conditions were pretty chaotic. Down in Nottingham, on the first Saturday in September 1914, a young man named Harry Fellows and two of his pals volunteered to join the cavalry: '…I do not claim that my

Sergeant W.F. Horn.
(Photo: T. Hewitson)

wish to join along with all those other young men came solely from love of my country … I would say that it was more for the need to feed and clothe myself than any degree of patriotism …' Only the infantry was available and the recruiting sergeant wanted them to join the Nottinghamshire and Derbyshire Regiment, whose depot was at Normanton Barracks in Derby. One of the lads said: '… we could walk to Derby, let's have a long train ride instead … so that is how we joined the Northumberland Fusiliers, as simple as that!'

In his unpublished memoirs Harry Fellows writes:

> We were given a railway warrant and some other papers and were instructed to report to the N.F. Barracks near St James' football ground on the Monday following. When we arrived at Victoria Station on that morning we found another half dozen lads who were about to make the same journey. I have no idea which route we took, only that we had at least four changes and did not arrive in Newcastle until late in the evening. When we eventually did arrive at our ultimate destination we found the barrack square was occupied by at least 2,000 men who were just sitting or walking about, each holding a blanket.
>
> Asking for instructions from one of these men we were told to go and hand our papers in at a window on the far side of the square. Following these instructions we found ourselves the possessors of a blanket and then it was every man for himself. None of us had had anything to eat since breakfast but we could see that there was no possible chance of getting anything there and, as the only way we knew in Newcastle was the way back to the (Central) station it was there we wandered to, to find at least 100 men who had the same idea as ourselves and like us, were wandering about with blankets over their shoulders. When night was falling, around nine o'clock, a kindly porter came up to us and told us that there were some

No. 3 Troop, A Squadron, the Northumberland Hussars leaves Newcastle in 1914. They are passing the bottom of Clayton Street West. (Photo: Imperial War Museum)

empty railway coaches standing on the line outside the station; and it was in these coaches that we spent our first night in the army.

Going back to the barracks at first light on the following morning we found that the crowd had increased in numbers and that the same lack of organisation was in evidence. The plain fact was that the rush to join the forces had taken everyone by surprise and the army was not organized to deal with such an influx. On our way back from the station someone had suggested that we should at least try to acquire some form of drinking vessel, but, although even at that early hour quite a few of the shops were open, everyone seemed to have run out of receptacles of any kind. Looking around the barrack square it was quite easy to see why! Men who had been wiser than ourselves were walking around with all kinds of receptacles, mugs, cups, vases, in fact anything that would hold liquid. Many of them had tied string through the handles and were carrying them bandolier fashion around their shoulders.

After a little while some movement was noticed from the direction of the cookhouse and men were seen carrying huge zinc baths filled with tea, which they deposited in the middle of the square. There was then a mad rush around the rear of the cookhouse by those who had no utensils in the hope of finding any empty food tins which could be of use. Some were lucky! others had to wait until they could borrow something from the more fortunate men.

Along a wall on one side of the square some trestle tables had been erected holding large clothes baskets filled with very thick hunks of bread and NCOs were seeing that the men queued to obtain one each. After obtaining the bread they were moved along to other tables where cooks stood holding large tablespoons with huge jars of jam in front of them. As each man passed a spoonful of jam was dumped on his bread and that was his breakfast. Afterwards it was just another sit, or walkabout, until about 3 p.m. when the same baths were brought out filled with stew, meat, carrots, turnip and potatoes; some men were actually seen rolling up their sleeves and diving their hands into the mess in search of meat.

During the day fresh arrivals were coming in all the time and it was now getting more uncomfortable to walk about. During the late afternoon volunteers were called for to join Winston Churchill's Royal Naval Division. About 50 men answered the call. Towards late evening 250 of us were lined up willy-nilly and marched off to some unknown destination in the town, where we eventually found we were in a place called Tilly's Assembly Rooms, which, I believe, was in Grainger Street.[4]

Harry Fellows eventually finished up in the 12th (Service) Battalion, the Northumberland Fusiliers, and took part in some of the most ferocious battles of that catastrophic war.

From the hordes of recruits who flocked into the barracks, eight service battalions of the Northumberland Fusiliers: 8th, 9th, 10th, 11th, 12th, 13th, 14th and 15th, were formed for Kitchener's Army; 1,800 men went to the 3rd (Special Reserve) Battalion of the Regiment, 500 to the Marines and Naval Reserve, and 1,400 to the Yorks and other regiments. The band of the 1st Battalion, the Northumberland Fusiliers, under Bandmaster Windram, was attached to the Regimental Depot, and the band of the 2nd Battalion, the Northumberland Fusiliers, under Bandmaster Cooper, was attached to the 3rd (Special Reserve) Battalion, the Northumberland Fusiliers. This battalion, whose headquarters had moved into the barracks from Alnwick, after the Haldane reorganisations of 1908, moved out to Canning Street Schools in Newcastle, then from there to East Boldon, and Scott's House, in West Boldon; in which places the battalion remained as a training unit until 1918.

By the end of January 1915, nearly all the Kitchener Battalions formed in the barracks had been recruited, organised, and despatched to various locations around the country where they joined their respective Brigades and Divisions. In that month a further 440 men were sent to the 3rd (Special Reserve) Battalion, the Northumberland Fusiliers. Colonel Dashwood of the Northumberland Fusiliers, had been appointed as commanding officer of the Fusilier Depot, and commander of troops in Newcastle Garrison. Captain Hall of the Northumberland Fusiliers had been appointed as adjutant to the depot and garrison. In the Fusilier Depot, Major White was officer commanding No. 1 Company, Major Short, officer commanding No. 2 Company, Major Norman, quartermaster, and Major Thomson recruiting officer. Regimental Sergeant Major E.E. Brindley was Depot Regimental Sergeant Major. A large proportion of the

Fusilier depot staff were time expired soldiers of the Regiment who had volunteered for war service, and were well over age.

No. 1 Company of the Fusiliers was billeted in the long barrack block ('U' Block), and No. 2 Company was living in the married quarters block, from which the families had been moved, and in fourteen huts which had been set up on the Leazes. Seven hundred men were in the Fusilier Depot. Recruiting went on at a furious rate, at an average of 1,000 men a month. By July, bell tents had been erected in the streets around the barracks to house the volunteers. Two-hundred and thirty wounded men from France and Belgium, who were recuperating, were living in the married quarter block. One of the wounded men was Private J. Comerford, from the 1st Battalion, the Northumberland Fusiliers. He had first joined the army in 1879, and had served with the mounted infantry at the battle of Majuba Hill, in South Africa in 1881, and served until 1896. He volunteered on 12 August 1914 and was sent to France with the 1st Battalion, the Northumberland Fusiliers. Wounded in April 1915, at St Eloi in Belgium, he had been sent back to England to recuperate. He would have been about fifty-nine years of age at this time.[5]

September 1915 saw a falling off in the numbers of men coming forward to serve. The Earl of Derby was appointed by the Government as Director of Recruiting, and he instituted a new scheme to boost recruiting. This 'Derby' scheme started in October 1915. Men were asked to attest their willingness to serve and to await their call up. The intention of this system was to try to avert conscription. If enough single men did not attest they would be conscripted before married men were called up. Probably one of the first men to join under the 'Derby' scheme was W.G. Jeffcock, whose home was in Newburn, Northumberland. According to his unpublished manuscript diary he ' ... enlisted at Newcastle Barracks [sic] in the RGA on 23 October 1915, left for Dover on 30 October ...' He eventually became 64414 Gunner W.G. Jeffcock, 91 Siege Battery, Royal Garrison Artillery. By December the 'Derby' scheme had not produced sufficient men, so the first Military Service Act, limited to single men under forty-one years of age, was passed within a month. It was not until March 1918 that the full Conscription Act was passed.

Those 'Derby' men who had enlisted under this system started reporting to the barracks. At this time a number of the sergeants who were in the barracks were posted to the newly raised 2nd (Garrison) Battalion, the Northumberland Fusiliers, which had its headquarters in the Hindbough (sic) Buildings, in Percy Street. This battalion sailed for Mesopotamia (Iraq), in February 1916, and eventually served in India. Of the recruits other than the 'Derby' men, 163 were posted to the 3rd (Special Reserve), and 15th (Reserve) Battalions, the Northumberland Fusiliers. 'Derby' recruits went, in the main, to the Royal Engineers, Army Service Corps, Royal Artillery and territorial battalions; some were sent to labour battalions.

With the end of the war in November 1918, a war in which over 16,000 officers and

TZ858 Able Seaman J.R.M. Wood. 2 Platoon, 'A' Company, Collingwood Battalion, whose home was in Newbiggin.

A large number of men who had volunteered for Kitchener's New Army transferred to the Tyne Division, Royal Naval Volunteer Reserve. They were placed in the Naval Division.

(Photo: T. Hewitson)

men of the Northumberland Fusiliers had lost their lives, and many, many more thousands had been maimed, a prolonged rundown of the war machine began. General demobilisation and the disbandment of war raised battalions got under way and the barracks became a dumping ground for regimental equipment such as band instruments, and other impedimenta from the service battalions, as well as regular soldiers who were hoping to continue their career in the army and awaiting regimental postings. It was not until 9 January 1920 that the last of the war-raised battalions of the Northumberland Fusiliers came home, when four officers and seven NCOs, the cadre of the 2nd (Garrison) Battalion, the Northumberland Fusiliers, arrived at the barracks from India.[6]

In February 1920, recruits for the 39th Battalion, the Northumberland Fusiliers, poured into the barracks from all over the country. So crowded was the depot that one company, which was 600 strong, had to be accommodated in the huts which had been built on the Leazes during the war. However, only two drafts left for France then the rest had to be sent to Ripon for demobilisation.[7]

Silk Union Flags, for the 9th, 10th, 11th, 16th, 18th, 19th, 20th, 21st, 24th, 26th, 27th, 51st, 52nd, 53rd, 1st and 2nd (Garrison) Battalions, the Northumberland Fusiliers, which had arrived at the depot during the year, and the old Colours of the 2nd Battalion, the Northumberland Fusiliers, were paraded on the Town Moor on 24

July 1920, then marched to St Nicholas Cathedral where they were laid up. Most of these Colours can still be seen hanging in the cathedral. The 25th and 26th Battalions' Colours were laid up in St Mary's Roman Catholic Cathedral, however, they are no longer displayed there.[8]

The 20th Battalion, the Northumberland Fusiliers, (1st Tyneside Scottish) silk union flag, which has recently been restored, can be seen in Ryton Parish Church; the 21st Battalion's (2nd Tyneside Scottish) is in St Cuthbert's Church, in Bedlington, the 23rd Battalion's (4th Tyneside Scottish) is in the Methodist Church in Jesmond. The 22nd Battalion's (3rd Tyneside Scottish) flag is among the large number of the remaining service battalions Union Flags of the 1914-18 War which can still be seen in St Nicholas Cathedral in Newcastle.

This phase, which lasted well into 1922, was further complicated by the recall of reservists due to the coal miners' strike in 1921, which lasted three months, and other social, industrial and political unrest throughout the country in that year. There was a very real fear of revolution among certain sections of the population of the country at this time. Men who had virtually just left the depot after demobilisation were recalled and many others, among them unemployed ex-soldiers, volunteered for the newly raised Defence Force. This force, based in the barracks, territorial army drill halls and other military establishments, was to be used for the defence of key points, and as an aid to the civil power, in the event of civil unrest. The force was only in existence for a short period.

A postcard sent to Mrs Whirly of Whitley Bay, from her son George, to say that he had arrived back in Blighty and was going to Newcastle Barracks. (Postcard: T. Hewitson)

6 Lean Years and the Geddes Axe
1920-1939

The two infantry depots and artillery units in the barracks gradually reverted to their pre-war role of training recruits for their respective regiments, and slipped back into the peacetime routine. Other events, however, had caused a great deal of consternation, not only within the units based in the barracks but in the armed services generally, prompting many regular servicemen to ponder upon their future. Great reductions in manpower after the end of the war were inevitable, but then, as now, much controversy was provoked by the severity of the defence cuts. Lloyd George, Liberal Prime Minister, appointed Sir Eric Geddes as chairman of a committee to achieve cuts of about £86,000,000 in public expenditure. The army's strength was to be cut by 50,000 officers and men. The anti-war sentiment after the slaughter of the Great War had become anti-services.[1]

Army Order 133 of April 1922, the 'Geddes Axe', stated that sixteen regiments of cavalry would be merged to form eight new regiments, and the Irish infantry regiments were to be disbanded on 31 July 1922 – the Royal Irish Regiment, the Royal Irish Fusiliers, the Connaught Rangers, the Prince of Wales Leinster Regiment, the Royal Munster Fusiliers, the Dublin Fusiliers. In November of that year King George V saw fit to cancel the disbandment of the Royal Irish Fusiliers. These reductions had a spin-off that benefited the Northumberland Fusiliers as six officers and 107 soldiers from the disbanded Irish infantry regiments volunteered to transfer to the Regiment.[2] One of them, John Ratcliff from the Dublin Fusiliers, was caretaker of the Royal Northumberland Fusiliers Regimental Museum in the barracks as late as 1958.

It was during the early 1920s that the barracks began to be referred to as Fenham Barracks. The 5th/68th officers' mess was finally moved into the 20th century with the installation of electricity in August 1924. This replaced gaslight and candles as a source of illumination. Another innovation was the fitting of a gleaming white bath which caused a great deal of excitement!

Class 'A' Reservists of the Northumberland Fusiliers were mobilised in the depot on 25-26 January 1927, and fifty were sent for service in China with the 1st Battalion, the Cameronian Scottish Rifles. These reservists were demobilised in the barracks on 21 October of the same year. A further party of thirty-four were released on 14 December.

Their Majesties King George V and Queen Mary visited Newcastle on 10 October 1928, to open the new Tyne Bridge. A Guard of Honour composed of fifty recruits from the Northumberland Fusiliers Depot, and fifty recruits from the Durham Light Infantry Depot, with the band of HMS *Helicon*, Tyne Division, the Royal Naval

Volunteer Reserve, was mounted at Jesmond Station to greet the royal party. The Guard was commanded by Captain J.H. Hogshaw MC, and Second Lieutenant R.C. Stockley of the Northumberland Fusiliers, and Lieutenant C.E.S. Phillips MM, of the Durham Light Infantry. After inspecting the guard, the Royal party proceeded to the new bridge where Guards of Honour were mounted by Tyne Division, the Royal Naval Volunteer Reserve and the 6th (City) Battalion, the Northumberland Fusiliers (TA).

During 1928 a start was made on the setting up of a Regimental Museum for the Northumberland Fusiliers in the barracks. This was situated on the first floor of the Institute Block, above the cobbler's and tailor's shops.

At the North East Coast Exhibition of 1929, which was opened by His Royal Highness the Prince of Wales, and following a suggestion from Dr. Bilbrough, the Lord Bishop of Newcastle, a small church hut was erected adjacent to the Palace of Arts, where visitors could rest, meditate and pray, if they so desired. After the exhibition was over all the units in the garrison contributed to a fund to purchase the hut which was then erected on the artillery parade ground in the barracks and consecrated as a garrison prayer hut by the Lord Bishop of Newcastle on 22 September 1930.

The North East Coast Exhibition was notable for the emphasis placed on musical entertainment. Captain H.G. Amers TD, the musical director for Eastbourne Corporation, and for many years associated with volunteer bands in the North East, notably the Northumberland Hussars, was appointed as Honorary Musical Director for the exhibition. He brought with him the Eastbourne Orchestra. In the specially

OPENING OF THE TYNE BRIDGE, 10th, OCTOBER 1928, by
His Majesty The King. D.

The King inspects the Guard of Honour. Soldiers line the new Tyne Bridge on 10th October 1928 as King George V and Queen Mary arrive for the opening ceremony.

70th Field Battery on parade in the artillery square in the early 1930s. The Riding school is on the left, and the Barracks Hospital is on the right. (Photo: Royal Artillery Historical Trust)

built Festival Hall, which sat 1,400 visitors, no fewer than fifty-four orchestral concerts were given to packed houses. Equally popular were the brass band contests sponsored by the *Newcastle Chronicle*. As in Newcastle's past, the military bands caused the crowds to flock to their performances in the arena.

The following list of regimental bands, quartered in the barracks during their engagements at the exhibition, shows how recent drastic economic cutbacks have affected present day military bands, compared with 1930: the Royal Horse Guards (The Blues), the 6th Dragoon Guards, the Grenadier Guards, the Coldstream Guards, the Welsh Guards, the Scots Guards, the Northumberland Fusiliers, the Green Howards, the King's Own Yorkshire Light Infantry, the Seaforth Highlanders, the Cameron Highlanders, the Royal Marines (Chatham Division), the Royal Air Force, Royal Artillery (TA), Royal Garrison Artillery (Tynemouth) (TA), Royal Artillery, 72 Field Brigade (TA), the Northumberland Hussars (TA), 6th Northumberland Fusiliers (TA), 8th Durham Light Infantry (TA), 9th Durham Light Infantry (TA).[3]

On 6 November the band and drums of the 1st Battalion, the Northumberland Fusiliers, were based in the barracks. During their stay the band played in the City Hall, and over the following week carried out a wide ranging series of engagements in the area of Newcastle.

In October 1932, a young Newcastle lad named Charles 'Chuck' Chambers, enlisted at the barracks for the Northumberland Fusiliers. He related that: 'We did six months training at the depot in Fenham Barracks. Some of the things we used to do were a bit ridiculous. Every Wednesday we used to be marched over the road to the

A bunch of likely lads of the Northumberland Fusiliers in PT dress, parading outside their billet in 'U' Block (Photo: C. Chambers)

Garrison Sports Ground, placed in a long line across the ground, then we had to slowly move across it digging out weeds with our table forks.'

Chuck also talked about the Soldiers' Home in Hunter's Road, and being marched out of the barrack gates, down Hunter's Road, and into St Luke's Church Hall for Padre's hour and religious instruction. He served in the Regiment for twenty-six years, and saw active service during the 1939-45 war, the Korean War 1950-51, and the Mau-Mau uprising in Kenya 1953-55, ending his service as a Warrant Officer class II.[4]

On Saturday 5 November 1932, the band and drums of the 2nd Battalion, the Northumberland Fusiliers, stationed at York, arrived in the barracks to spend a week fulfiling engagements in the Newcastle area. On Sunday morning they played the depot to church and were accompanied back to the barracks by a large crowd who listened to the band playing on the barrack square. In the afternoon a composite Guard of Honour of the Royal Naval Volunteer Reserve, Royal Artillery, the Northumberland Fusiliers and the Durham Light Infantry, attended at the City War Memorial in Eldon Square, and the Corps of Drums played the British Legion and the civic party from the service in St Nicholas Cathedral to the memorial.

The visit created a lot of local interest and a film company took the opportunity of

Recruits of the Durham Light Infantry Depot on Inkerman Day, 1933. (Photo: Harry Moses)

filming the band and drums during their stay in Newcastle. On Tuesday afternoon, 8 November, the band and drums beat Retreat on the square. It is reported that an estimated 6,000 visitors watched the performance. Two days later, on Friday 11 November, the civic party and a composite Guard of Honour formed up at Barras Bridge, and led by the band and drums marched to the Eldon Square Armistice Ceremony. An extremely large crowd was at the ceremony and during the two minutes silence the *St George's Gazette* reports that a party of Communists tried to create a disturbance in the Bigg Market and they only just missed a rough handling by the crowd.

To mark his Silver Jubilee, King George V granted the Royal prefix to the Northumberland Fusiliers on 3 June 1935, Army Order 110/1935. From that date the Regiment was to be designated as the Royal Northumberland Fusiliers, and was allowed to retain the gosling green facing colour of the Regiment instead of the royal blue facing colour normally worn by Royal Regiments.[5]

An 'At Home' was held in the barracks on 24 July 1935, which was visited by 45,000 people. The band of the 2nd Battalion, the Royal Northumberland Fusiliers from York, played during the course of the afternoon. In the September of 1935, Orderly Room Quartermaster Sergeant (ORQMS) Len Letchfield, of the Durham Light Infantry, retired after twenty-seven years service; of which period he had spent sixteen years at the depot. He was to be landlord of the Spital House, a pub just out of the back gate of the barracks.

His Majesty King George V died in January 1936, and the proclamation of His Majesty King Edward VIII took place outside the Moot Hall on 23 January. A detachment of recruits from the 5th/68th Depots, commanded by Second Lieutenant

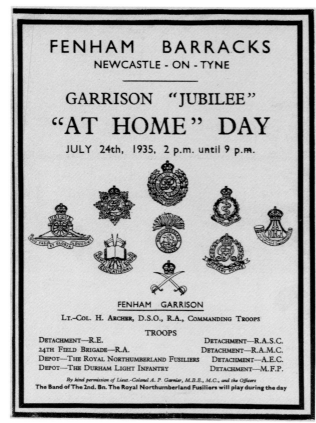

An advertisement for the 'At Home' of July 1935.

Townsend, of the Durham Light Infantry, along with troops from the Royal Artillery, formed a guard for the Town Clerk reading the proclamation. In June meetings took place to discuss a five year plan for the reconstruction of the barracks. The Artillery Riding School, officers' mess and barrack block were to be demolished and modern 'Sandhurst' type blocks would replace them. However, the start of the Second World War put a stop to much of the new development.

Recruiting for the newly formed Supplementary Reserve began in September 1936. This was restricted to single men aged from seventeen to twenty-five who would enlist for six years. They were to do twenty-six weeks training in the first year, fourteen weeks at the Regimental depot, then twelve weeks with the home based battalion of the Regiment. For the following five years they would do an annual training camp of fourteen days. They could re-enlist for four years at a time after the first six. This would obviously only have an appeal for unemployed young men who did not want a permanent career in the army. Fenham Barracks was the first depot in the area to start this scheme and it coincided with an 'At Home' held by all the units in the garrison. This event took place on 2 September 1936 and was an outstanding success; 52,000 people visited the barracks between the hours of 2 p.m. and 8.30 p.m. The Royal Air Force, members of the Red Cross, St John's Ambulance Brigade, and the Durham Light Infantry Army Cadets, took part in the various exercises and displays that were organised.

Due to civil unrest by Arab extremists in Palestine, the 2nd Battalion, the Royal Northumberland Fusiliers was ordered to that country. Class 'A' Reservists of the Regiment were recalled and thirty-four men reported to the Fusilier depot in the barracks on 5 September. They then moved on to the 2nd Battalion at York.

The Jubilee Parade on the Town Moor, 1935. The Royal Northumberland Fusiliers march past the Lord Mayor.

Following the abdication of His Majesty King Edward VIII in 1937, the proclamation of His Majesty King George VI took place outside the Town Hall in Newcastle, where a detachment of troops from the joint depots under Second Lieutenant J.J.B. Jackman, of the Royal Northumberland Fusiliers (who was to be awarded a posthumous Victoria Cross for his heroism on 25 November 1941, at Tobruk in North Africa) took part in the ceremony. A detachment from the Royal Artillery in the barracks, and the band of the Newcastle City Police Force were also in attendance.

In January 1937, the Fusilier depot began training on the Vickers medium machine gun. New army regulations came into force in April under which recruits would no longer have to purchase such items as regimental canes, extra gym shorts and shoes, and padlocks for their lockers. These items would be issued and would make a saving of 6s. 6d. (32 ½ pence) for the recruits.

To mark the Coronation of His Majesty King George VI, a review was held on the Town Moor in which 1,200 troops from the Newcastle Garrison, and 1,100 ex-servicemen took part. Coronation medals were awarded to the following permanent staff of the Royal Northumberland Fusiliers depot; officer commanding Major Hogshaw, Lieutenant (Quartermaster) Redhead, Regimental Sergeant Major (RSM) Curtis and Fusilier Cassidy.

Civilian employees in the barracks were mainly ex-servicemen. In August 1937 there were three employed as dining hall orderlies, and one as bath-house orderly and sanitation duty-man. Joseph Kelly had served eight years with the 2nd Battalion; John Atkinson Malia, seven years with the 1st and 2nd Battalions; Lawrence McDonald, seven years with the 2nd Battalion; and Peter McKenna, had served eight years with the 1st and 2nd Battalions. They were all former Fusiliers.

The Cruiser HMS *Newcastle* sailed into the River Tyne in October 1937 for the purpose of being presented with a silver ship's bell by the Lord Mayor, on behalf of the citizens of Newcastle upon Tyne. While the ship was berthed by the Quayside it was open to visitors, and teams from the ship's crew took part in many sporting events against teams from the troops in the barracks.

Following the move of the Royal Artillery units in the barracks to Dunbar, in January 1938, work on the renovation of the barracks finally began in April, with the demolition of the Royal Artillery build-ings which were to be replaced by Sandhurst block. In May the Royal Artillery cookhouse and the .22 indoor rifle range were demolished. On Thursday 7 July 1938, the Lord Mayor of Newcastle, Alderman Gilbert Oliver, accompanied by Major General Herbert, Colonel of the Regiment, the Royal Northumberland Fusiliers, laid the foundation stone of the first 'Sandhurst' block. A Guard of Honour for this occasion was mounted by recruits from the Royal Northumberland Fusilier and the Durham Light Infantry Depots in the barracks, a contingent from the Royal Artillery at Otterburn, and veterans of the South African War. Also playing at the ceremony was the band of the 9th Battalion, the Durham Light Infantry (TA).

By June 1939 a new gymnasium was in use and a wooden hutted Militia camp was being built, on land requisitioned by the War Office, on the opposite side of the road from the barracks next to the Garrison Sports Ground. This camp was situated in an area bounded by Ponteland Road, Brighton Grove, Nun's Moor Park, and Studely Terrace. The camp was eventually handed over to Newcastle Corporation in 1956, and the hutments were demolished.

7 *World War II and after 1939-1996*

In May 1939 a limited form of conscription was introduced by the Government. The first batch of conscripts from the 'Militia scheme' for the Royal Northumberland Fusiliers reported to the barracks in July 1939, and the regular recruits in the depot were sent to the 2nd Battalion at Dover to make room for them. The recruits very probably did not return to Fenham, but went to France with the 2nd Battalion as part of the British Expeditionary Force.

This scheme had to be supplemented later, and this led to the introduction of the National Service (Armed Forces) Bill on 2 September 1939 under which all able bodied men between the ages of eighteen and forty-one were eligible for military service: ' ... for the duration of the hostilities ... '. As part of the build up of the Territorial Army, 40 Company, the Women's Auxiliary Territorial Service (ATS) started drill nights and training in the barracks; this company was commanded by a Mrs Ramsden.

With the outbreak of the 1939-45 war, great changes took place among the units based in the barracks. The depot of the Durham Light Infantry left the barracks for its new quarters in Brancepeth Castle, County Durham. The Royal Northumberland Fusilier depot was reorganised as a machine gun training centre under Major H.F. Attwater until August 1941, when the training centres of the various machine gun reg-

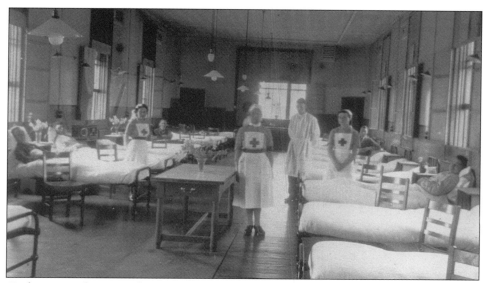

Fenham Barracks Hospital in 1940, after Dunkirk. The hospital is reputed to be the last Florence Nightingale hospital in the British Isles.

iments of the British Army were concentrated at Chester. All the regimental property was moved into the Armoury Tower Block by the main gate into the barracks and a small depot party was left in the barracks under the command of Major D.C. Bucknall. From 1942, regimental depots stopped training recruits for their respective regiments and all recruits went into the General Service Corps, where they were trained in newly formed Army Basic Training Centres. At this stage the barracks complex was in a state of confusion due to the renovation work that had started in 1938 and the married quarters had all been vacated.

The barracks were then used as a training centre for women of the Auxiliary Territorial Service (ATS), who were accommodated in the newly built Sandhurst Block. In 1943, the 11th (Royal Jersey Militia) Battalion, the Hampshire Regiment, was also stationed in the barracks. The former married quarters were used as offices by the battalion. The band was quartered in the old artillery block, the companies in 'U' Block, and the sergeants' mess was in the Institute Block at the north end of the infantry square. The officers' mess was just behind Sandhurst Block, and an assault course was built over the road in the Militia Camp.[1] Small detachments of support units such as the Royal Army Ordnance Corps, Royal Army Service Corps, and various branches of the army were accommodated in the barracks throughout the war.

By the end of the war the barracks were in a dilapidated state with large parts unoccupied until No. 5 County Primary Training Centre was opened on 9 December 1946, under the command of Lieutenant Colonel B. Tarleton, of the Royal Northumberland Fusiliers, for the training of conscripts. This was the first time in the history of Great Britain that conscription had been introduced in peacetime, apart from a few months in 1939. The last intake of recruits into this training centre arrived on 19 February 1948, and the centre officially closed on 31 March 1948. Recruits were then trained at the Yorkshire and Northumberland Brigade Training Centre at Strensall Barracks near York.

All that was left in the barracks at Newcastle was a Regimental Cadre of four officers and fourteen warrant officers, non-commissioned officers and fusiliers, with the Regimental band under Bandmaster Evans attached. This cadre, with its role not finally decided, moved into a wing of Sandhurst Block. During this period 990 Company, the Royal Army Service Corps moved into the barracks and took over half of Sandhurst Block and responsibility for garrison duties. This company was redesignated as 59 Company, RASC, on 2 August 1952.[2]

April 1948 was a busy time for the Royal Northumberland Fusiliers in the barracks. The Freedom of Berwick upon Tweed, was granted to the Regiment on 21 April, and the Freedom of Newcastle upon Tyne on 23 April. Most of the hundred men of the Regiment who took part in the ceremonies in Berwick and Newcastle, came from the depot at Fenham and the Infantry Training Centre at Strensall. On Sunday 11 July 1948, the cadre of the 2nd Battalion, the Royal Northumberland Fusiliers, arrived from Gibraltar. The battalion was finally to be disbanded on 1 August 1948, by the simple expedient of changing its number from 2 to 1, thus reactivating the 1st Battalion, which had been placed in suspended animation in 1946. It was during this period that Mr G.N. Farrier was appointed as Honorary Curator of the Regimental Museum in the barracks

In January/February 1949, 81 Heavy Anti-Aircraft Regiment, Royal Artillery, moved into the barracks from Sandy Lane Camp at Gosforth on the outskirts of Newcastle. On 23 April, at a ceremony attended by representatives of the Old Comrades Association and detachments from the 4th Battalion, the Royal Northumberland Fusiliers (TA), 588 Light Anti-Aircraft Regiment, Royal Artillery (formerly 5th Battalion RNF) (TA), 43rd Royal Tank Regiment, (formerly 6th (City) Battalion RNF) (TA), and the 7th Battalion, the Royal Northumberland Fusiliers (TA), with the Corps of Drums of 588 L.A.A. Regiment, RA (TA), the old Colours of the 2nd Battalion, the Royal Northumberland Fusiliers, which had been presented to the

A squad of national service recruits in No. 5 Primary Training Centre, Fenham Barracks 1947. Sergeant 'Chuck' Chambers, the squad sergeant is seated in the centre row. Note the 'General Service' bakelite cap badges which were worn until a recruit was posted to a regiment. Also note the extreme youth of the recruits. (Photo: C. Chambers)

battalion at Sabathu, India, on 14 May 1914, were laid up in the Regimental Museum in Sandhurst block.

On Sunday 12 February 1950, Her Royal Highness the Princess Royal visited the barracks to inspect the local territorial army battalion of the Women's Royal Army Corps (WRAC), of which she was Controller Commandant. After inspecting the battalion and presenting medals, she visited the depot and museum of the Royal Northumberland Fusiliers. In the next month Captain J.L. Baume, Adjutant of the depot, was selected to play for the English rugby team against Scotland in the Calcutta Cup match on Saturday, 18 March 1950.

An illuminated Roll of Honour Book and lectern, for those of the Royal Northumberland Fusiliers who had lost their lives during World War II, were dedicated in St Nicholas Cathedral on Sunday 23 April 1950. Detachments from the 1st and 7th Battalions of the Regiment stayed in the barracks over the weekend. In June, headquarters of 151 Infantry Brigade (TA) moved into the barracks. In August, 200 officers and men of the 3rd Battalion, the Coldstream Guards, with their band, were accommodated in the barracks. They were in Newcastle to take part in the tercentenary celebrations of the raising of their Regiment.

With the departure of the 1st Battalion, the Royal Northumberland Fusiliers to Korea on 11 October 1950, the Regimental band arrived at the depot with the Colours, which were to be lodged in the officers' mess, and the battalion's baggage which was to be stored at the depot until its return.

After a decision by the War Office to allow regimental depots to start training recruits for their respective regiments, the first National Servicemen for the depot of the Royal Northumberland Fusiliers arrived on Thursday, 15 November 1951. Fifty-eight conscripts reported, and with twelve regular recruits two squads of thirty-five each were formed. Recruit Company was once again housed in 'U' Block, which looked onto the infantry square. Training of National Servicemen and regular recruits for the regiment began; at least that was the theory, unfortunately the War Office had other ideas. The National Servicemen of the first intake were posted to the York and Lancaster Regiment in Austria, as was the second intake.

Following the death of His Majesty King George VI on 6 February 1952, the proclamation of Her Majesty Queen Elizabeth II was read outside the Town Hall by the Town Clerk on 8 February 1952. A detachment of one officer and thirty men of 81 Heavy Anti-Aircraft Regiment, Royal Artillery, the depot, the Royal Northumberland Fusiliers, with the band of the 1st Battalion, and one officer and forty men of the Royal Air Force were on parade for the occasion.

On Saturday 11 October 1952, 500 officers and men of the 1st Battalion, the Royal Northumberland Fusiliers, arrived at the barracks from their base at Brancepeth, County Durham, to take part in a civic reception given by the Lord Mayor of

Newcastle upon Tyne, Alderman Mrs V.H. Graham, and the Corporation and citizens of the city, to mark the return of the battalion from Korea. After marching through the city the battalion went to a luncheon in the Old Assembly Rooms. The next day, after spending the night with some in Fenham Barracks, and some in the militia camp across the road, a Memorial Service was held in St Nicholas Cathedral.

Every six weeks, groups of apprehensive young men would walk in through the barrack gates and report at the guardroom to begin their period of National Service. Many of these young men saw this as a disruption to their chosen careers, some looked upon it as a diversion before starting their adult life, while others saw it as an imposition on their freedom of choice. In the main, however, the young National Serviceman completed his service without too much trouble. After all, the 1939-45 War was over and the world was supposed to be at peace! However, many of them saw active service in Malaya, Korea, the Canal Zone, Kenya, Suez and Cyprus; some of them losing their lives in the process.

At 11.00 a.m. on Thursday, 17 September 1953, a not so raw recruit, Thomas Lee Hewitson, a twenty-one year old from Ashington, Northumberland, who had been deferred from call-up at the age of eighteen to complete his apprenticeship, reported at the barracks to commence his two years National Service with the Royal Northumberland Fusiliers. He had been a member of the Northumberland Army

A group photograph of 'Y' Squad taken in the gymnasium after passing out in December 1953. The majority were national servicemen, with a few three-year regulars. Most were posted to the 1st Battalion, the Northumberland Fusiliers in Kenya, where they spent the rest of their two years service. The author is seated third from the right in the front row.

(Photo: T. Hewitson)

Cadet Force from the age of thirteen, becoming a sergeant and gaining War Office Certificate 'A' Parts I & II, followed by nearly three years service in the Territorial Army. He had always had a desire to be a regular soldier and he considered himself a shade better prepared than the average recruit. He also saw National Service as a way to discover if he and the army were compatible. He was quite looking forward to the new experience.

After reporting to the guard-room at the gate to the barracks, where the corporal asked me if I was a reservist as I was wearing my territorial army uniform, and full field service marching order, the first thing we did was to go into a room where we were documented by a team of clerks. We were issued with Part I and Part II paybooks, and ten shillings (50 pence) as an advance from our pay of four shillings (20 pence) per day. This was not a humanitarian gesture I might add. On a large blackboard was chalked a long list of items that we had to purchase from the NAAFI canteen, yellow dusters, blanco (khaki-green), metal polish (Brasso), boot polish, coathangers and many other items; the ten shillings did not last long! 'Y' Squad, as we were now designated, was later marched to the quartermaster's store in the Armoury Tower where uniforms and equipment were issued. As I had brought my TA uniforms and equipment with me I had to wait until the next day to have a kit check and be issued with anything that I was deficient of.

The next day Sergeant W. Beattie, my squad sergeant, took me to the QM's for my kit check. The first thing I had to exchange was my pair of gym shoes. They were white, and as the issue at the depot was black I had to have a black pair. Imagine my surprise when the first words my squad corporal said to me when I returned to the barrack room were: 'get those f.....g sandshoes blancoed white!' It was then that my first doubts about being a soldier stirred.

Many other ludicrous and seemingly incomprehensible practices, allied with the humiliating scenes enacted on the barrack square that took place over the succeeding weeks, which all seemed to be aimed at destroying the confidence and natural rebelliousness of youth, hardened my views against regular service; but the clincher was the supper in our first week of training. Sergeant Beattie told us that as recruits we were entitled to a supper meal. The bulk of the squad put their names down in the supper-book, much to the annoyance of the duty cook, a ginger haired lance corporal of Scottish origin, whose job it was to see that we were fed that night. At about 7.30 p.m. we trooped over to the cookhouse for our meal. I don't know if you have ever eaten cold kippers, with very lukewarm, unsweetened cocoa. If you haven't, don't! Some of us said that we did not want it; the cook's reply was: 'you wanted your f—.g supper, so you'll f—g well eat it! ... I'll teach you b—s to book suppers and keep me back in this f—g cookhouse!' I think he must have been a National Serviceman! Suffice it to say, none of us ever booked a supper meal again.[3]

We endured the polishing, blancoing, and 'bulling' of boots to a mirror like finish, the

*Fusilier Tommy Hewitson, 'Y' Squad Recruit
Company, Royal Northumberland Fusiliers,
October 1953.*

(Photo: T. Hewitson)

generally pointless 'spit and polish', the liberal applications of floor polish, for which each recruit had to donate one shilling (5p) towards the cost, and the lavish use of 'Jet Glaze' (an intense, black, gleaming lacquer) on shovels, bayonet scabbards, the rubber binding around the sides of our gym shoes after we had blancoed them white, spare leather bootlaces that had to be rolled up into circles, like the liquorice we used to buy as children – which meant we had to buy another pair of laces in case we needed them – and anything else that the NCOs thought needed to be black and shiny. This lacquer was sold by Woolworths for use on the old fashioned black kitchen ranges, still prevalent in the 1950s, for those who did not want to use black-lead.

A lot of these practices died out with the introduction of the 1958 pattern equipment with blackened metal buckles etc. which did not need 'blanco' along with anodised aluminium badges and buttons which did not need polishing. The metal polish and 'blanco' manufacturers must have lost a fortune. The ending of National Service in 1960 and the introduction of an all regular army, with the realisation that things would have to change if regular recruits were to be recruited – and kept – led to a more liberal regime and sounded the death knell for the old fashioned attitudes of many of the senior officers and NCOs of the regular army of that time.[4]

8   The Fusilier Brigade and the Royal Regiment of Fusiliers

As part of the changes in the composition of the army in 1958, the three English Fusilier Regiments: the Royal Northumberland Fusiliers (5th Foot); the Royal Fusiliers (City of London) (7th Foot); the Lancashire Fusiliers (20th Foot); were formed into the Fusilier Brigade, wearing insignia common to the three regiments. A new cap badge, buttons, collar and shoulder badges were designed to incorporate various elements of the three old regimental cap badges, and on 9 January 1958, in the drill shed of a snow covered Fenham Barracks, Mrs D.A. Fitzpatrick, Lord Mayor of Newcastle, presented the officers, warrant officers and a sergeant from each of the three regiments with the new cap badge at a rebadging ceremony. However, the three distinctive hackles worn by the Fusilier Regiments: red over white for the RNF, white for the RF, and primrose for the LF, were retained.

From 1958 junior bandsmen and drummers for the new brigade were trained in the barracks, then from December 1961, recruits from the three old regimental recruiting areas were trained there. The last Fusilier Brigade recruits left the barracks in July 1962, for a new Fusilier Brigade Depot at Sutton Coldfield, near Birmingham.

A colourful and impressive military ceremony, which was shown live on local television, took place in the barracks on Saturday 30 September 1961. On a wet morning, with the rain glistening on the tarmac, the Northumberland Hussars (TA), received a new Guidon. It was presented to the Regiment by the Duke of Northumberland KG, Lord Lieutenant of the County of Northumberland, a former officer of the Regiment, and whose younger brother, Lord Richard Percy, was the commanding officer. The Regiment was organised into two guards dressed in No. 1 dress blues with Cambridge blue piping, white metal chain-mail epaulettes, and white metal buttons and badges. A squadron in the

The Armoury Tower and the guardroom c.1966. The Armoury housed the Regimental Headquarters, the Northumberland Fusiliers. It also housed the Regimental Museum. A small detachment of regular soldiers from the 1st Battalion was attached to the headquarters for recruiting purposes.

The former guardroom, on the left, was where recruits would book in and out, where prisoners would be kept in cells, and those recruits on 'Jankers' (defaulters parade) would fall in at various times of the day from early morning to late evening, where they would be drilled or detailed for fatigues. Many recruits saw the interior of the guardroom, sometimes for very trivial offences. (Photo: T. Hewitson)

rear in khaki battledress mounted in landrovers and scout cars, and the Regimental bands of the Northumberland Hussars and the 15/19th Hussars in No.1 dress blues, with the scarlet-topped caps of the 15th/19th provided a vivid splash of colour. The Guidon party consisted of Squadron Sergeant Majors W.A. Willis (Guidon), J.W. Siddle and W. Cole. Three officers of the Regiment, Messrs Cookson, Charlton and Murray, mounted on horseback, enlivened the scene wearing pre-1914 full dress uniforms with gleaming saddlery and leopard skin shabraques on their superb horses – a magnificent display of colour and pageantry which lit up the infantry square of the barracks on that damp and dismal morning, and a wonderful sight for the 1,500 spectators who watched the presentation.[1]

What was to be the last occasion that the Royal Northumberland Fusiliers marched together as a Regiment through Newcastle, took place on Saturday 6 August 1966. The 1st Battalion was at Otterburn, Northumberland, on intensive training preparing for service in Aden, and the opportunity was taken to exercise the right of the Regiment to march through the City of Newcastle with bayonets fixed, drums beating and Colours flying, which had been granted on 18 February 1948.

The Regiment, consisting of the 1st Battalion, with its Colours, Band and Drums; the 4/5th Battalion (TA) with its Colours, Band and Drums; the 6th (City) Battalion

(TA) with its Colours, Band and Drums; and the 7th Battalion (TA) with its Colours, Band and Drums; and a large contingent of the Royal Northumberland Fusiliers Comrades Association, formed up on the infantry square in the barracks. The whole Regiment then marched through the City, with the battalions in order of precedence, via Barrack Road, Wellington Street, Bath Lane, Westgate Road, Grainger Street, past Grey's Monument, Blackett Street, Eldon Square (the saluting base), Percy Street, then Claremont Road into the Exhibition Park on the Town Moor. The parade was also part of Newcastle Army Week which was being run in conjunction with the Newcastle Summer Festival. After arriving on the Town Moor the battalions were dismissed to their various locations. The massed bands and drums of the Regiment carried out the ceremony of the Beating of Retreat in front of a massive audience that same evening. This was the first and last time that the Royal Northumberland Fusiliers exercised its right to march through the City of Newcastle upon Tyne as a complete Regiment

The band and drums of the 6th (City) Battalion, led by Drum Major Black, march down City Road 6th August 1966. This was the first and last occasion when the Royal Northumberland Fusiliers marched through Newcastle as a complete Regiment. (Photo: T. Hewitson)

The Royal Regiment of Fusiliers

As part of the army reforms of that period, on 23 April 1968, (St George's Day) a new large regiment was formed from the four battalions of the Fusilier Brigade, which by now included the Royal Warwickshire Regiment, (6th Foot) and it was designated as the Royal Regiment of Fusiliers. The Royal Northumberland Fusiliers, as the senior regiment, became the 1st Battalion of the new regiment. Various alterations were made to the insignia worn by the Regiment, and the red over white hackle of the Royal Northumberland Fusiliers was adopted by all battalions of the new Regiment.

A presence was maintained in the barracks by the Regimental Information Team, and Regimental Headquarters (Northumberland), the Royal Regiment of Fusiliers, commanded by Captain (Retired) W.P. Pringle MBE, until 1990, when the Fusilier element finally severed the regiment's connection with Newcastle's own barracks and the headquarters moved to Alnwick, where it was co-located in Fenkle Street, with the Headquarters of the 6th (Northumberland) Battalion, the Royal Regiment of Fusiliers (TA). For a few months the Regimental Information Team occupied two rooms in Sandhurst Block, but they eventually moved to St George's Drill Hall, a Royal Regiment of Fusiliers TA Centre, in Sandyford Road.

A new training centre was built in the barracks on the site of the old married quarters to house the Northumbrian Officers Training Corps, and this was opened in 1991. The Territorial Army still maintains a presence in the barracks with Headquarters of the Queen's Own Yeomanry (formerly the Northumberland Hussars), reformed in January 1971, the unit moved into Sandhurst Block in the barracks in 1977, and home Headquarters of the Light Dragoons (formerly 15/19th Hussars) a regular army unit, is also resident in this block. The Royal Army Medical Corps (TA) also maintains a unit in the barracks, No. 201 Field Hospital.

It was reported in the *Evening Chronicle* of 26 March 1982, that the Corporation intended to demolish the two original entrance guardrooms, built in 1806, and reputedly designed by James Wyatt the distinguished architect. This was opposed by Mr Peter Guillery of the Georgian Society, and the Ministry of the Environment later rejected the Corporation proposal. A public house and restaurant, the Inn On The Park was eventually built, incorporating the two gatehouses, and opened on 3 December 1986.[6] This public house was later closed, but reopened as the Cushy Billet.

Following the latest forces review and the subsequent reductions in Territorial Army units, it will be interesting to see what eventually happens to the old barracks, which for nearly two hundred years have played such an important part in Newcastle life.

Regiments of the British Army associated with the Barracks in Newcastle from 1806

The following list of regiments has been compiled from primary and secondary sources, which include contemporary press reports, regimental journals, official service records, and personal and oral accounts by soldiers who served in the barracks. For references in other printed sources I have given the author's surname which can be found in the bibliography. Every unit listed has a reference verifying its presence in the barracks, and for brevity I have used the following abbreviations for the various sources.

(NC): *Newcastle Courant*
(NDC): *Newcastle Daily Chronicle*
(NJ): *Newcastle Journal*
(NA): *Northumberland Advertiser*
(TM): *Tyne Mercury*
(SGG): *St George's Gazette*
(RAHT): *Royal Artillery Historical Trust*
(HAL): *Hart's Annual Army Lists*
(JSAHR): *Journal of the Society for Army Historical Research*
(NAM): *National Army Museum*
(SUSM): *Scottish United Services Museum*
(RHQ): *Regimental Headquarters*
(ILN): *Illustrated London News*
(NCL): *Newcastle City Library*
(DC): *Depot Companies*

The barracks were originally built as a depot for artillery and cavalry. Unfortunately, although numerous references to artillery detachment in the barracks appear in the local press when they took part in ceremonies in Newcastle, it has not been possible to find the designation of these units until the 1870s; it would appear that major formations of the Royal Artillery were based in the barracks from then.

Without the assistance of Brigadier K.A. Timbers, and officers of the Royal Artillery Historical Trust at Woolwich, the artillery list which follows would have been very difficult to compile.

Royal Artillery

1873/74: D. I. K. Batteries, 14 Brigade, Royal Field Artillery. (RA)

1874/77: A. C. G. E. Batteries, 16 Brigade, RFA. (RAHT)

1877/80: I. Battery, 4 Brigade, RFA. (RAHT)

1880/81: N. Battery, 4 Brigade, RFA. (RAHT)

1880/82: A. Battery, 4 Brigade, RFA. (RAHT)

1882/83: J. Battery, 1 Brigade, RFA. (RAHT)

1882/84: Depot Battery, 2 Brigade, RFA. (RAHT)

1882/84: Depot Battery, Northern Division, Royal Artillery. (RAHT)

1883/84: G. Battery, 3 Brigade, RFA. (RAHT)

1884/85: X. Battery, 1 Brigade, RFA. (RAHT)

1884/89: Depot Battery, 1 Brigade, RFA. (RAHT)

1889/93: 62 Field Battery, RFA. (RAHT)

1889/90: 33 Field Battery, RFA. (RAHT)

1890/92: 56 Field Battery, RFA. (RAHT)

1891/94: 66 Field Battery, RFA. (RAHT)

1892/95: 73 Field Battery, RFA. (RAHT) & Baron.

1893/96: 63 Field Battery, RFA. (RAHT)

1894/97: 7 Field Battery, RFA. (RAHT)

1895/99: 74 Field Battery, RFA. (RAHT)

1896/98: 14 Field Battery, RFA. (RAHT)

1897/99: 84 Field Battery, RFA. (RAHT)

1898/99: 86 Field Battery, RFA. (RAHT)

1900/02: 110. 111. 112. Batteries, 24 Brigade, RFA. (RAHT)

1900: 7 Division Ammunition Column, RA. (SGG)

1902/04: 43. 86. 87. Batteries, 12 Brigade, RFA. (RAHT) & Baron.

1904/07: 128. 129. 130. Batteries, 30 Brigade, RFA. (RAHT)

1907/09: 37. 61. 65. Batteries, 8 Brigade, RFA. (RAHT) & Baron.

1909/13: 27. 36. 60. Batteries, 35 Brigade, RFA. (RAHT)

1913/22: 136. 137. Batteries, No. 1. Reserve Brigade, RFA. (RAHT)

1921: 501. 502. Batteries, No. 1. Reserve Brigade, RFA. (RAHT)

1924/27: 10 Field Brigade, Royal Artillery. (RAHT)

1927/29: P. Y. Z. Q. Batteries, 21 Field Brigade, RA. (RAHT)

1929/31: 29. 39. 96. 97. Batteries, 19 Field Brigade, RA. (RAHT)

1932/36: 22. 50. 56. 70. Batteries, 24 Field Brigade, RA. (RAHT)

1936/38: 6. 23. 49. 91. Batteries, 12 Field Brigade, RA. (RAHT)

1951/54: 81 Heavy Anti-Aircraft Regiment, RA. (SGG)

The Royal Artillery moved out of the barracks in 1938 due to the demolition of some of the old barrack blocks occupied by them, and the start of what was to be a programme of modernisation put into effect by Hore-Belisha, the War Minister. Unfortunately, the start of the 1939-45 war stopped the work and the only new building finished was Sandhurst Block, now occupied by Territorial Army units. In 1951, 81 HAA Regiment moved from Sandy Lane Camp, Gosforth, to the barracks.

Cavalry Regiments

There were generally detachments of cavalry stationed in the barracks, ranging from one troop up to a squadron. Headquarters of a cavalry regiment was usually at York, with individual troops of the regiment scattered all over the north of England. For instance: in June 1848 the 1st the Queen's Dragoons arrived in England from Ireland. Regimental Headquarters was in York and detachments were sent to Bradford, Halifax, Leeds and Newcastle.

In 1861 the 3rd, 4th, 7th, 13th, 18th, 19th, 20th and 21st Light Dragoons were retitled as Hussars.

1806/07: The North British Dragoons. (NC) 19 March 1806.

1807/09: 6th (Inniskilling) Dragoon Guards. (NC) 17 January 1807.

1810: 4th (Royal Irish) Dragoons. (NC) 26 May 1810.

1812: 2nd Dragoon Guards. (NC) 6 June 1812.

1817: 13th Light Dragoons. (NC) 4 July 1817.

1817/20: 6th (Inniskilling) Dragoon Guards. (NC) 17 October 1818, (NAM) & Pease.

1820: 3rd Light Dragoons. (NC) 9 June 1820.

1820: 4th Dragoon Guards. (NC) 23 June 1820.

1824/25: 1st The Royal Dragoon Guards. (JSAHR) Vol. LI. 1973, ppl-3.

1825/26: 3rd Light Dragoons. (NAM & NC) 12 May 1826.

1825/26: 7th (The Queen's Own) Light Dragoons. (NAM).

1826/27: 17th Lancers?

1828/29 1st The Royal Dragoons.

1829/30: 4th Dragoon Guards. (NC) 17 Oct 1829.

1830/31: 3rd Light Dragoons. (NC) 3 July 1830. (NC) 21 May 1831.

1833/34: 2nd Dragoons (Scots Greys). (NAM).

1834/35: 7th (The Queen's Own)Light Dragoons. (JSAHR) Vol. L. Autumn 1972. (NC) 18 April 1835.

1835: 6th (Inniskilling) Dragoon Guards. (NC) 18 April 1835.

1838/39: 5th Dragoon Guards. (NAM) & Cadogan.

1839: 7th Dragoon Guards. (NC) 2 August 1839.

1842/43: 17th Lancers. (NC) 21 October 1842.

1843/44: 8th (King Royal Irish) Hussars. (NAM).

1848/50: 1st The Queen's Dragoons.

1850: 2nd Dragoons. (NJ) 20 April 1850.

1850: 16th Lancers. (HAL) 1850 p153.

1851/52: 3rd Light Dragoons.

1853/54: 6th (Inniskilling) Dragoon Guards. (NJ) 7 May 1853.

1854/55: 7th (The Queen's Own) Light Dragoons. (NC) 9 May 1855.

1864: 16th Lancers. (HAL) 1864 p56.

1866/67: 4th Hussars. (NC) 26 April 1867.

1867: 14th Hussars. (NC) 26 April 1867.

1871: 7th (The Queen's Own) Hussars.(HAL) 1871.

1878: 2nd Dragoon Guards (Scots Greys). (HAL) 1878

Infantry Regiments

Once again space was a problem. The barracks were not large enough to house a complete infantry regiment before 1880. When a battalion was posted to the North East of England it was usually dispersed between Newcastle Barracks, Sunderland Barracks, Tynemouth Castle and outlying detachments. From 1825, twelve company infantry battalions were reorganised into eight service companies and four depot companies. When the service companies went overseas the depot companies remained in the United Kingdom, recruiting and training replacements for the service companies. Another function of the depot companies was that of acting as Aid to the Civil Power in the event of civil unrest and disasters.

A typical example of the deployment of a battalion on home service was the 26th Foot (The Cameronian Scottish Rifles). Three companies came to Newcastle on 19 August 1844. One company went to Thornley Hall and West Rainton; one for Durham and one to Whitridge Farm. Another party arrived on the 22nd, one company to Newcastle Barracks, one to Tynemouth Castle and two to Sunderland Barracks. Headquarters arrived in Newcastle Barracks on the 30th. On 24 April 1845, the regiment, less detachments at Tynemouth and Sunderland, left Newcastle by rail for Manchester.

The infantry units, or detachments of units which were resident in the barracks are listed by their date of occupation, precedence number at the time, and their Territorial designation after 1881.

1811: 82nd Foot. (2nd Battalion, The South Lancashire Regiment 1881). Sykes.

1816: 33rd Foot. (1st Battalion, The Duke of Wellington's Regiment 1881). Sykes.

1827: 4th Foot. (The King's Own Royal Regiment 1881). (TM) 19 June 1827.

1829: 80th Foot. (DC) (2nd Battalion South Staffordshire Regiment 1881). (NC) 19 September 1829.

1830/33: 19th Foot. (DC) (The Green Howards 1881). Calladine

1833: 24th Foot. (DC) (The South Wales Borderers 1881). (NA) 22 October 1833.

1838/39: 52nd Foot. (DC) (2nd Battalion. The Oxfordshire & Buckinghamshire Light Infantry 1881). (NC) 29 June 1838 & Cadogan.

1839/41: 98th Foot. (2nd Battalion, The North Staffordshire Regiment 1881). (RHQ) 24 February 1996 & (NC) 2 August 1839.

1841: 87th Foot. (DC) (1st Battalion, The Royal Irish Fusiliers 1881). (RHQ) 5 February 1996, (NC) 26 June 1841 & Sykes pp146-147.

1841: 10th Foot. (1st Battalion, The Lincolnshire Regiment

1881). (RHQ) 21 March 1996 & (NJ) 26 June 1841.

1841/43: 61st Foot. (2nd Battalion, The Gloucestershire Regiment 1881). (NC) 1 April 1843.

1843/44: 37th Foot. (1st Battalion, The Hampshire Regiment 1881). (RHQ) 12 February 1996 & (NC) 9 June 1843.

1844/45: 26th Foot. (1st Battalion, The Cameronian Scottish Rifles). (SUSM) 22 February 1996.

1845/46: 36th Foot. (DC) (2nd Battalion, The Worcestershire Regiment 1881). (NC) 3 May 1845.

1846/48: 30th Foot. (1st Battalion, The East Lancashire Regiment 1881). (NJ) 1 July 1848.

1848/50: 63rd Foot. (1st Battalion, The Manchester Regiment 1881). (RHQ) March 1996 & (NJ) 20 April 1850.

1850/51: 33rd Foot. (1st Battalion, The Duke of Wellington's Regiment 1881). (ILN) 7 September 1850. (NCL), Local History Items Vol. I.

1851/52: 21st Foot. (1st Battalion, The Royal Scots Fusiliers 1881). (RHQ) 23 April 1996 & (NC) 27 February 1852.

1852/53: 28th Foot. (1st Battalion, The Gloucestershire 1881). (NJ) 28 May 1853.

1853/54: 6th Foot. (DC) (1st Battalion, The Royal Warwickshire Regiment 1881). (NJ) 11 June 1853.

1854/55: 26th Foot. (1st Battalion, the Cameronian Scottish Sykes & Carter.

1855/57: 85th Foot. (DC) (2nd Battalion, The Shropshire Light Infantry 1881). (NC) 9 May 1856.

1857/58: 5th Fusiliers. (2nd Battalion, The Northumberland Fusiliers 1881). (NC) 26 February 1858.

1858: The Nottinghamshire Militia. (3rd Battalion, The Sherwood Foresters 1881).

(NC) 5 March 1858.

1858/59: The Rifle Brigade. (1st Battalion, The Rifle Brigade 1881). (NDC) 17 January 1859.

1860: 29th Foot. (DC) (1st battalion, The Worcestershire Regiment 1881).

1861/62: 58th Foot. (2nd Battalion, Northamptonshire Regiment 1881). (NC) 30 August 1861.

It is possible that the barracks had been unoccupied for some time, as the item in the *Newcastle Courant* is titled 'Reoccupation of the Newcastle Barracks.' This could have been due to renovations and rebuilding.

1862: 41st Foot. (1st Battalion The Welsh Regiment 1881). (NC) 31 January 1862.

1865/66: 85th Foot. (2nd Battalion, The King's Shropshire Light Infantry 1881). Barrett.

1868/69: 22nd Foot: (The Cheshire Regiment 1881). (HAL) 1868.

1869/71: 98th Foot: (2nd Battalion, The North Staffordshire Regiment 1881). Fordyce Vol. II.

1871/72: 35th Foot: (1st Battalion, The Royal Sussex Regiment). (SUSM) 22 February 1996 & (HAL) 1871.

1871: 73rd Foot: (DC) (2nd Battalion, The Black Watch 1881). Depot Company attached to 35th Foot. (SUSM) 22 February 1996.

1881: 5th Fusiliers. (The Northumberland Fusiliers 1881). Regimental Depot set up as part of the 5th/68th Regimental District.

1883: The Durham Light Infantry. Regimental Depot moves from Sunderland Barracks to Newcastle Barracks and sets up depot as part of the 5th/68th Regimental District.

Other Units

1900: Elswick Battery, Royal Artillery (Volunteers).

1900: 14th, 15th, 55th, Squadrons, Northumberland and Durham Imperial Yeomanry. Pease.

1900: Volunteer Service Sections, Northumberland and Durham Volunteer Battalions. (SGG) 1900.

1939: 40 Company, Auxiliary Territorial Service (TA) (SGG) 1939.

1939: Auxiliary Territorial Service (ATS), training centre formed in the barracks and accommodated in Sandhurst Block. Oral account former Major D. Woodford, late

The Hampshire Regiment.

1943/44: 11th (Royal Militia Island of Jersey) Battalion, The Hampshire Regiment. (RHQ) December 1996, & Oral account by former Major D. Woodford, late The Hampshire Regiment.

1947/48: No. 5 County Primary Training Centre. (SGG) 1947 & oral account by former Warrant Officer II. C. Chambers, late The Royal Northumberland Fusiliers.

1951: 990 Company, The Royal Army Service Corps. (SGG) 1951& (RHQ) 12 February 1996.

1952: Headquarters 151 Brigade, 50th (Northumbrian) Division (TA). (SGG) 1952.

1956: Headquarters 151 Brigade, 50th (Northumbrian) Division (TA), redesignated as 149 Brigade. Balcer & Rust.

1957/59: The Royal Army Pay Corps. (RHQ) 13 February 1996.

1958: The Fusilier Brigade. An amalgamated depot to train recruits for the newly formed Fusilier Brigade was set up in place of The Royal Northumberland Fusiliers Depot. (SGG) April 1959.

1962: Regimental Headquarters, The Royal Northumberland Fusiliers. (SGG) 1962.

1967: Headquarters 29 Engineer Brigade transfer from Edinburgh and established in the Institute Block

1968: The Royal Regiment of Fusiliers formed April 23rd 1968. Regimental Headquarters (Northumberland) The Royal Regiment of Fusiliers set up in the barracks. (SGG) 1968.

1979: The Queen's Own Yeomanry occupied Sandhurst block 27/28 November, co-located with Home Headquarters 15th/19th Hussars (Oral account R. Thompson).

Appendix – Doreen and Sergeant Bill Beattie

Sergeant Bill Beattie, 1st Battalion, the Royal Northumberland Fusiliers, was posted to the Regimental Depot at Fenham Barracks after his return from Korea, where he had served from November 1950 to November 1951. He was placed on the depot staff as a squad sergeant training National Service and Regular recruits. He served in the barracks until he was posted back to the 1st Battalion in 1954, which at that time was in Kenya taking part in the Mau-Mau campaign. His wife Doreen, who lived with him in married quarters in the barracks, wrote the following description of the quarters they occupied in the barracks, and the facilities available to the married families.

Bill returned from Korea in December 1951 and was posted to the Depot, Fenham Barracks in early January 1952. I arrived in Newcastle in early May '52 with our son Robert. It was quite cold, although the soldiers were in shirt sleeve order, and I thought what a terrible place, quite austere.

My first quarter was in Ack-Ack Block, No. 5.(AA). My next door neighbours were the Olivers – he was Regimental Quartermaster Sergeant at that time. Considering the age of the barracks and the buildings, my quarter was quite nice inside and with hindsight was probably a palace compared to what many people in civilian life had to live in. The quarter comprised of: downstairs a living room (approx. 12ft by 12ft) and a kitchen. Upstairs, there was one bedroom and a bathroom.

Furnishings in the living room were two armchairs, dining table, four chairs, sideboard, a built in cupboard by the fireplace and a badly worn carpet covering most of the floor leaving a wooden surround, highly polished of course. Decoration was cream distempered walls and white glossed woodwork. The kitchen was a reasonable size with walls of unplastered brick, with the top half of the walls distempered cream and the dado painted army green gloss; the doors were painted army green also. It was fairly well equipped with a large sink, hot and cold running water and a gas clothes boiler, and a pulley to hang the wet clothes on and raise up to the ceiling to dry. I think the dining table and two chairs were always in the kitchen as space was at a premium.

Upstairs we had a bedroom with double bed, two bedside lockers (other ranks for the use of), and wardrobe. We had our own cot but I think they were available if needed. All soft furnishings and utensils were provided – except cutlery. We were not allowed to decorate unless we put it back to its original state before moving out; expensive in those days.

The main source of heating and hot water was the coal fire in the living room. Coal was delivered each week on a Tuesday in winter. The rent and cost of coal and electricity was deducted from Bill's pay before he got it. We were, of course, still under rationing and the bulk of our purchases were made at the NAAFI shop, with our day to day shopping in Spital Tongues.

After our second son was born 12 March 1953, we moved into a two bedroomed flat in 'W' Block. Other than the fact that the rooms were larger, the layout, furnishings etc. were the same. I can't remember the number now but we were about three from the NAAFI. Both units, Royal Artillery and Royal Northumberland Fusiliers, shared both types of quarters so we were mixed.

There was no clinic as such and no Medical Officer, the soldiers were looked after by a civilian doctor whose practice was in Spital Tongues, although he used the MI room and the MRS with an army staff and an Royal Army Medical Corps staff sergeant. The wives were mostly patients of a Dr. Millar, who had a surgery opposite the General Hospital. The Midwife was a Mrs Nicholson who delivered young Bill at home and also visited on a regular basis. There was no other medical care available until about a year later when the new maternity unit was opened at the General.

I can't remember any article in the papers about NCOs swearing, nor any incident of this type that involved Bill. Bill always used to talk about the women, mostly Royal Artillery families, who used to lie out of the windows of 'W' Block laughing and making fun of the recruits making mistakes at drill. Bill and Duggie Gardner used to regularly march their squads to the north corner of the square, turn them to face 'W' Block and tell recruits in a loud voice that the women would be better employed cleaning their dirty houses than laughing at them. The Adjutant, Captain Kierney, sent for Bill on several occasions over this matter but nothing was ever done about it as far as I know.

Other Fusilier families who lived in quarters at that time, mainly bandsmen, were: Olivers (Vic & Edna); Baileys (Peter & Joy); Tomlinsons (Stan & Kath); Hewitsons (? & Dot); Hazelgreaves (Bill & ?), band; Colcloughs, band; Christies, band; Shells (Jock & ?) Regimental Sergeant Major; St Quentins (? & ?) Orderly Room Quartermaster Sergeant; Strakers, band; McKennas; Boyles (Ned & ?); Timmusses, Army Physical Training Corps; Huggins (Dave & ?) Recruiter Coldstream Guards; and Major 'Jehu' Brown, the Quartermaster.

The Institute Block. 'D' Block, under the clock.

This was partly the NAAFI and was empty, although Recruit Company used it from time to time as an indoor training area. The Royal Artillery Sergeants' Mess was next door. The RNF Sergeants' Mess moved back into there at the end of the '50s. The Fusilier Depot Sergeant Mess was next to the Armourers' shop, on the right as you came through the main gates into the barracks.

The RA shared 'U' Block occupying about two thirds of it. The RNF band was in Sandhurst Block, including the band store and practice room. Also in the block were the Orderly Room, Officer Commanding depot office, Adjutant's and RSM's offices. The Depot Holding Platoon also had accommodation in the block. Part of the block was used as offices for the Royal Artillery.

Note and References

Chapter 1

1: Public Record Office, HO42/25 - 201-202.

2: Sykes, John, *Local Records*, Volume 2, 1866. Republished Patrick & Shotton 1973, p2.

3: Public Record Office, pp1854/5, XXXII, 37. *Report from an Official Committee on Barrack Accommodation for the Army.*

4: Biehan, John, *Archaeologia Aeliana*, 'Army Barracks in the North East in the Era of the French Revolution', Fifth Series, Volume XVIII, pp165-176.

5: Adjutant-General, General Regulations and Orders for the Army, Adjutant-General's Office, Horse Guards. William Clowes, London 1822, pp207-208.

6: Hewitson, Thomas, Personal recollections.

7: Ferrar, Naj. M. L. (ed) *Colour Sergeant George Calladine's Diary 1793-1837*, E. Fisher, London 1922, p185.

8: Calladine, George, Op cit. p190.

9: Calladine, George, Op cit. p190.

10: Cadogan, Peter, *Early Radical Newcastle*, Newcastle 1975.

11: St George's Gazette 1898. 'History of the 2nd Battalion, the Royal Northumberland Fusiliers 1857 - 1859' p72.

12: Newcastle Council Reports 1873/74, pp69-80-111.

13: Newcastle Council Reports 1876/77, pp254-271-348-356-374-393.

14: Op cit. pp254-271-348-356-374-393.

15: Op cit.

Chapter 2

1: *St George's Gazette*, 'Before Our Time', Colonel W. F. Way Dover, January 1942, p18.

2: *St George's Gazette*, 'Depot Notes', Dover, January 1884, p3.

3: Taylor, Olive, *Bygone Spital Tongues*, Newcastle City Libraries & Arts, Newcastle 1993, p8.

4: *St George's Gazette*, 'Depot Notes', Dover, May 1893, pp70-71.

5: *St George's Gazette*, 'An Account of the march of the 2nd Battalion through Northumberland', Dover, August 1889, pp129-135.

Chapter 3

1: Cookson, Col. J.B., Colonel of the Northumberland (Hussar) Yeomanry, Mitford Hall, Northumberland.

2: Elphick, Lt. Col. G. Joined the Yeomanry as a private in June 1871, became veterinary officer in 1878. When the 1914-18 war started he was 65 years of age, but he raised and trained a veterinary company for the Northumbrian Territorial Division. Subsequently acted as Assistant Director of Veterinary Services with the rank of Lieutenant Colonel.

3: Spurgin, K. B. *On Active Service with the Northumberland and Durham Yeoman*, pp1-4.

4: Middlemiss, George, *With the Northumberland Volunteers in South Africa*, pp3-6.

5: Fraser,. John, *Sixty Years in Uniform*, pp188-190.

6: Digest of Service: Services of the 4th Battalion Northumberland Fusiliers from February 1900 to Disbandment December 1906

7: Wearmouth, Robert F., *Pages from a Padre's Diary*, pp12-13.

Chapter 4

1: *St George's Gazette*. Extract from the 'Alnwick & County Gazette' of 7 March 1908, quoted p44.

2: *St George's Gazette.*'Laying up of the Colours of the Third and Fourth Battalions of the Fifth Fusiliers, and the Unveiling of the Northumbrian War Memorial', Dover 1908, pp98-104.

3: *St George's Gazette*. 'Laying Up of the Colours of the First Battalion, Fifth Fusiliers', Dover 1914, pp31-33.

Chapter 5

1: Newspaper account, *Blyth News & Wansbeck Telegraph*, 14 September 1914.

2: Beatty, George, Oral recording in the author's collection.

3: Horn. W.F.,. *St George's Gazette*. February. Dover 1918, p17.

4: Fellows, Harold, Unpublished account from 'The Fellows Papers', in the author's collection. Courtesy of his son.

5: Comerford, J., *St George's Gazette*. 'Depot Notes', June, Dover 1915, p104.

6: *St George's Gazette*. 'Depot Notes', January, Dover 1920, p8.

7: *St George's Gazette*. 'Depot Notes', February, Dover 1920, p20.

8: *St George's Gazette*. 'The Northumberland Fusiliers, Laying Up of Battalions' Colours', 'Depot Notes' August, Dover 1920, pp104-106.

Chapter 6

1: Brereton, J.M., *The British Soldier*, p144.

2: Ed. *St George's Gazette*. pp198-99.

3: Lambert, *Newcastle's Spacious Year*.

4: Chambers, C., An oral recording made on 27 September 1996, in the author's collection.

5: Wood, Col. D.R., *The Fifth Fusiliers and its Badges*. p1.

Chapter 7

1: Woodford, D., Oral evidence of Major Woodford, who served in the 11th (RJM) Battalion, The Hampshire Regiment, in Fenham Barracks during the 1939-45 War.

2: Warden, J. T., Letter from the assistant curator of the museum of The Royal Logistic Corps, 12 April 1996.

3: Hewitson, T. L., Personal recollections.

4: Hewitson, T. L., In 1959 Company Sergeant Major W. Beattie, my former squad sergeant, was posted as an Permanent Staff Instructor to the TA unit in which I was serving as a National Service Volunteer: 'B' Company, 7/ Battalion, the Royal Northumberland Fusiliers (TA).

Chapter 8

1: Bastin, J., *A History of the Northumberland Hussars 1945 - 1983*, Pages 50, 51 & 52.

2: Ed. North East Times. Photographs and an account of the opening event appeared in the January 1987 issue of the publication.

Further Reading

Barclay, C.N.   *The History of the Royal Northumberland Fusiliers in the Second World War.*, London, 1952.

Baron, F.   *The Town Moor Hoppings, Newcastle's Temperance Festival 1882-1982,* 1984.

Beihan, J.   'Army Barracks in the North East in the era of the French Revolution', In *Archaeologia Aeliana*, Fifth Series, Vol XVII.

Brereton, J.M.   *The British Soldier 1661 to the Present Day*, Bodley Head, 1986.

Colls, R.   *The Pitmen of the Northern Coalfield*, Manchester University Press, 1987.

Farwell, R.   *Queen and Country*, Allen Lane, 1981.

Ferrar, M.L.   *The Diary of Colour Sergeant George Calladine 1793-1837*, Eden Fisher & Co., 1922.

Fraser, J.   *Sixty Years in Uniform*, Stanley Paul & Co., 1939.

Hoy, M.   *Bygone Fenham*, Newcastle City Libraries, 1988.

Latimer, J.   *Local Records or Historical Register of Remarkable Events which have occurred in Northumberland, Durham, Newcastle upon Tyne and Berwick upon Tweed 1832-1857*, Chronicle Office, 1857.

March, G.   *Flames Across the Tyne*, E.F. Peterson & Son, 1974.

Spurgin, K.B.   *On Active Service with the Northumberland and Durham Yeomanry South Africa 1900-01*, Walter Scott Publishing, 1902.

Sykes, J.   *Local Records or Historical Records of Northumberland and Durham, Newcastle upon Tyne and Berwick upon Tweed*, 1866, 2nd edn. Patrick & Shotton, 1973.

Taylor, Olive   *Bygone Spital Tongues*, Newcastle City Libraries, 1993.

Vane, W.L.   *The Durham Light Infantry*, Gale & Polden Ltd., 1914.

Wearmouth, F.   *Pages from a Padre's Diary*, Ramsden Williams Publications, 1950.

Index of Armed Services and personal names in the text.